ROADBLOCKS

ROADBLOCKS

Spiritual Challenges in Islamic Work

VOLUME I

Adapted and translated from
Aafat 'ala at-Tariq

As-Sayyid Muhammad Nuh

MAS PUBLISHING

Published by MAS Publishing
712 H Street NE, Suite 1258
Washington, DC 20002
www.muslimamericansociety.org

Copyright @ 2021 by Muslim American Society (MAS)
1st Edition August 2021

ISBN 978-0-9792113-4-8

Printed in the U.S.A

CONTENTS

Roadblocks was translated and adapted from the first volume of the Arabic series *Aafaat 'ala at-Tareeq* by Shaikh As-Sayyid Muhammad Nuh, first published in 1987. May Allah shower His mercy and blessing upon the author whose scholarship and insight continue to enlighten today.

MAS Publishing hopes this adapted translation serves well its intended audience—young American Muslims who are interested in dedicating their lives to working for Islam. Translation decisions are the subjective result of weighing meanings, context, priorities, and intended audience. Some Arabic terms are used in the text, defined upon their first usage. A glossary of commonly used Arabic words in the book can be found on the next page. In order to provide a work that is more relevant and relatable to readers, we have added commentary in the form of text features and, in some cases, modified examples to be more relevant and added quotations from actual workers in the field. As with other MAS Publishing titles, the present work is an adapted translation rather than a strictly literal one.

Abdelminem Mustafa was the lead translator, along with a team of volunteers that spent many hours editing, revising, and adding commentary to the rough translation. This volume was generously sponsored by a MAS member—may Allah be pleased with her and shower her parents and family with blessings and forgiveness.

ABOUT THE AUTHOR

As-Sayyid Muhammad Nuh (1946-2007) was a prolific scholar and writer of Egyptian descent. A world-class professor of Hadith Sciences at Al-Azhar University, Shaikh Nuh visited and lectured at universities around the world. Shaikh Nuh was passionate about the fields of dawah and collective Islamic work, and wrote more than 20 books on these topics and others. Respected by even those who disagreed with his dynamic, practical approaches, Shaikh Nuh is lauded among circles of scholars as a man of perfected prayer and great humility, who keenly listened to the youth and favored action over theory.

GLOSSARY

Allah: the Arabic name for God

Ansar: the native inhabitants of Medina who believed in and supported the Prophet and the migrants from Mecca (Muhajiroon)

Athan: the call to prayer

Ayah: a verse of the Quran

Companions: Those who converted to Islam and lived alongside Prophet Muhammad ﷺ

Dawah: invitation; the mission of calling others to worship God and follow Islam

Dua: supplication or prayer; the act of calling upon God

Fitrah: the initial state of creation of a person; the collection of attributes and tendencies the human was initially given

Futoor: spiritual burnout, slackening, loss of momentum; having once been active and then slowing down or dropping out

Hadith: a saying of Prophet Muhammad ﷺ transmitted through a chain of narrators. The sayings and traditions of the Prophet were meticulously recorded and verified after his death.

Hadith qudsi: a saying of the Prophet Muhammad ﷺ in which he conveys a statement of God

Iman: translated as faith, belief. Derived from *'amn* (safety), *iman* linguistically means taking something as true, accepting it, and believing in it. In Islam, *iman* is belief, action, and intention stemming from certainty and complete acceptance of the existence of God and His attributes, and the Prophet and revelation. Iman is not only expressed in the heart, but also through worship, good deeds, and intentions. It can increase and decrease, and its strength or weakness reaches the depths of the self and affects all its aspects.

Insha'Allah: God willing

Jama'ah: a group or community that works together; the congregation, the majority; sometimes used in context of the Islamic movement.

Muhajiroon: emigrants; Muslims from Mecca who migrated to Medina

Nafs: the self, ego; may be inspired with good or evil tendencies

Naseehah: sincerity, advice, and counsel. Encompasses many meanings, the common thread being sincerely wishing well for others.

Quran: the final revelation from God to all of mankind, sent through Prophet Muhammad

Riya': showing off, seeking admiration of people

Salah: prayer; derived from *silah*, meaning connection; the fifth pillar of Islam

Salla Allahu alaihi wa sallam (ﷺ): This is a prayer meaning, "May God's peace and blessings be upon him."

Seerah: the biography of Prophet Muhammad

Sunnah: the way, course, or conduct of life; the example set by Prophet Muhammad which all Muslims should strive to follow as best as they can. It can also refer to extra acts of worship that one can perform in order to gain favor with God.

Surah: a chapter of the Quran

Tafseer: the science of explaining the Quran and deriving its rulings

Tarbiyah: the holistic development and nurturing of Islamic character

Thikr: remembrance of God

Ummah: the collective body of Muslims

Wudu: a ritual washing before prayer

Introduction

In the name of Allah, the Most Merciful, the Most Compassionate.
All praise is due to Allah. May His peace and blessings be upon Prophet
Muhammad, his family, and his Companions. May Allah's peace be upon all
those who follow the Prophet's path and invite to his message.

This book is the first in a series addressing the spiritual challenges facing Islamic workers. *Roadblocks* is unique in that it is not a general guide on Islamic spirituality and self-improvement—it is written for individuals who are already committed to working for the sake of God.

Whether you call yourself an activist, an Islamic worker, a community volunteer, or a caller to Allah, you understand that Islam is more than just an individual's faith—it is a life mission to call to the way of Allah and to work for the betterment of humanity. An Islamic worker adopts the call to Islam as their life's work, taking the practice of religion beyond the individual dimension, sharing it with families and communities, dedicating their time, money, and personal comfort for the sake of Allah, and joining hands with a mission-driven community to promote good and tide evil.

Travelers upon a road must prepare for their journey, equipping themselves and learning about the roadblocks they will encounter along the way. Working for Islam is the most blessed occupation we can take up in this life, but it is also a difficult road with forces scheming to drive us off course. Many roadblocks lie in wait, some the result of devilish schemes and others contrived by our own misdeeds. These roadblocks force weak and ill-prepared travelers to the wayside, sometimes causing them to abandon Islamic work entirely.

Roadblocks is an in-depth exploration of the spiritual diseases most commonly afflicting Islamic workers in their journey, roadblocks from without and within. Each chapter dissects the causes and symptoms of a specific spiritual disease, the effects on both the individual and the trajectory of Islamic work, and finally, equips the reader with a series of solutions and preventative measures.

Use this book to diagnose, understand, prevent, and treat. Use this book to help you remain steadfast on this path you chose, journeying behind the most blessed of footsteps, in the wisest of company, toward the greatest destination.

May Allah help you trek this path for the duration of your life, granting you guidance and the provisions of success: God-consciousness, patience, good company and foresight.

MAS PUBLISHING
AUGUST 2021

Spiritual Burnout

Futoor is defined in the Arabic dictionary as halting after being in motion, or to become lazy and listless after having been active and energetic. Here, in this guide to assessing and refining our souls in the context of Islamic work, we translated the word *futoor* as spiritual burnout, a common roadblock that afflicts almost every activist at some point during which he or she may slow down significantly or even drop out of Islamic work and the practice of good deeds. *Futoor* in this context can also be translated as slackening, reduced productivity, dropping out, laziness, or apathy.

Once active, driven, and positive, the individual infected by spiritual burnout becomes distracted from their original aims. Its mildest symptoms include laziness and lack of initiative, while the most severe symptoms are dropping out of Islamic work and neglecting the cause of Allah completely.

> "It creeps up on me when I go a long time without any kind of spiritual recharge. Maybe I get too busy, or maybe just lazy, but I stop connecting with my source of motivation. As my fuel tank grows emptier, I run on fumes and easy distractions, like reality TV, internet, and food. The most rewarding things in my life, like helping in my MSA and going to the mosque on Fridays start to feel cumbersome. I skip meetings, slack off, and easily grow frustrated with others. I even start asking myself questions like, 'What's the point? Nothing changes. I'm eventually going to fail anyway, so why keep working so hard?' It's a very slippery slope."

You might be experiencing spiritual burnout if:

✓ *Your responsibilities feel more burdensome than usual.* You have to drag yourself to perform in the field of Islamic work and are tempted to drop out of activities that were once a habit.

✓ *You are performing less worship than usual.* The five prayers, reading Quran daily, and performing basic acts of worship feel tedious. You are barely performing the minimum requirements.

✓ *You were once much more active.* Then, life shifted. Maybe you got a job, got married, graduated, moved to a different city, or had a disagreement with someone. You fell short of your former habits of activism and diligence.

✓ *You are cynical of the community and people who are working for Islam.* We all are familiar with this negative discourse and canceling of good works: "Leaders are bad, scholars are backward, organizations are useless, and no one is skilled, organized, or charismatic enough."

✓ *You waste a lot of time.* Once you spent much of your time volunteering, working, learning, and attending noble gatherings. Now the distribution of your time has shifted towards more self-centered preoccupations.

Burnout: Inside or out?

We typically understand burnout as physical and emotional exhaustion due to external stresses, but the Islamic concept of *futoor* encompasses more than this limited concept. Spiritual burnout is just as often caused by internal ailments, such as forgetting death and the afterlife, befriending the wrong people, misconceptions about life and Islamic work, or over-indulgence.

We easily recognize physical and mental burnout because of the weariness and sense of overwhelm it brings about; spiritual burnout can be more subtle, manifesting as decreased worship, withered vision, and a reluctance to volunteer effort or money for the sake of Allah. We can think of this decrease in commitment and momentum as burnout not only of the mind and body, but also of the heart.

A form of the word *futoor* can be found in the Quran. Allah describes the angels' ceaseless glorification:

وَلَهُۥ مَن فِى ٱلسَّمَـٰوَٰتِ وَٱلْأَرْضِ وَمَنْ عِندَهُۥ لَا يَسْتَكْبِرُونَ عَنْ عِبَادَتِهِۦ وَلَا يَسْتَحْسِرُونَ ۝ يُسَبِّحُونَ ٱلَّيْلَ وَٱلنَّهَارَ لَا يَفْتُرُونَ ۝

To Him belong all those in the heavens and the earth. And those nearest to Him are not too proud to worship Him, nor do they tire. They glorify day and night, never <u>wavering</u>. [21:19-20]

In these verses, "never wavering" indicates that the angels are in constant worship, glorifying Allah and declaring His supremacy. They pray and mention Allah night and day, never waning or growing weary in their constant glorification.[1]

Causes of Spiritual Burnout

This chapter will explore a number of reasons that someone who was once actively engaged in community service and Islamic work can begin to disengage and burnout. They include:

- Overindulgence
- Isolation
- Forgetting death and the Afterlife
- Neglecting daily worship
- Consuming what is prohibited or unethical
- Focusing only on one aspect of religion
- Ignoring Allah's patterns and divine ways
- Physical exhaustion
- Lack of preparation for challenges
- Friends who drag you down
- Lack of organized priorities
- Belittling the effects of small sins
- Excessiveness in Worship

OVERINDULGENCE

Too much of something permissible—even something good—can be harmful and will cause spiritual burnout. Overindulgence leads to apathy, desensitization of the heart, obesity, and laziness. It is the main channel through which passion and desire overwhelm intellect and moral conscience. Even when it doesn't stop us from moving forward, overindulgence will slow us down and delay the achievement of our goals.

This might be the underlying reason for which Allah and His Messenger prohibited us from being excessive in any regard. Allah says,

$$يَـٰبَنِىٓ ءَادَمَ خُذُواْ زِينَتَكُمْ عِندَ كُلِّ مَسْجِدٍ وَكُلُواْ وَٱشْرَبُواْ وَلَا تُسْرِفُوٓاْ ۚ إِنَّهُۥ لَا يُحِبُّ ٱلْمُسْرِفِينَ ۝$$

Children of Adam! Dress properly whenever you are at worship. Eat and drink, but do not waste. Surely He does not like the wasteful. [7:31]

The Messenger of Allah ﷺ said, *"The human being does not fill any container worse than his own stomach."*[2]

The early generation of Muslims understood very well the dangers of excessiveness and warned against it. The Mother of the Believers, Aishah, observed, "The first test that happened to this nation after the Prophet's ﷺ passing was being full. When people's stomachs are full, their bodies grow fat, their hearts grow weak, and their passions grow wild."[3] These wise words of Aishah draw a connection between overindulgence and a weakened resolve and commitment to the mission. The great Companion Umar ibn al-Khattab once said,

> Beware of gluttony in food and drink, for it ruins the body, causes disease, and makes you too lazy to pray. Be keen on moderation, for it is better for the body and prevents excessiveness. Allah dislikes the fat scholar, and a person is not destroyed completely until he favors his desire over his religion.[4]

Numerous spiritual diseases can be traced to excess and overindulgence. An early scholar of the spiritual sciences, Abu Sulaymān al-Dārāni, said that there were six spiritual shortcomings connected to having a full stomach: lack of sweetness in speaking to Allah, the inability to retain knowledge, the loss of empathy for others, difficulty in performing physical acts of worship, the increase of lustful desires, and spending long amounts of time in places other than the mosque.

Indulgence in the Technology Age

There are dimensions to overindulgence that go beyond food and physical appetites. Our easy access to technology opens the door to all kinds of new indulgences, some forbidden and some not, but even those that are permissible are detrimental in large doses. The hadiths and sayings about overeating most certainly apply to these other forms of indulgence as well. Social media and entertainment outlets are meticulously designed to steal our time and sabotage our ability to focus. A Muslim community glued to their screens will be unable to uphold the mission entrusted to them. A lack of awareness and control over how we consume technology can easily cripple us as Islamic workers and harm the entire community.

ISOLATION

The road of working for Islam is a long one. There are many transitions, hills to climb, obstacles to overcome, and the results often seem beyond our reach. When we try to go it alone, isolated from the community, we will find it nearly impossible to stay constant and maintain momentum. There are no team members to remind us of Allah, supporting and cheering us on, renewing our vision and determination, inspiring us to stay firm. Alone, it is easy to grow fatigued and disinterested. When inevitable challenges arise along the road, the isolated, disengaged Muslim will slow down and feel dispirited, if not give up altogether.

This is why Islam stresses the importance of collective work and being part of a *jama'ah*, a mission-driven community. Mobilizing through organized work and journeying as a community for the sake of Allah around a direction and a mission is one of the highest forms of obedience to God.

Jama'ah: a group or community that works together; the congregation, the majority; sometimes used in context of an Islamic movement.

The Quran warns us against isolating ourselves, separating from the mission and vision of the community and going it alone:

وَٱعْتَصِمُوا بِحَبْلِ ٱللَّهِ جَمِيعًا وَلَا تَفَرَّقُوا

And hold firmly to the rope of Allah and do not be divided. [3:103]

وَتَعَاوَنُوا عَلَى ٱلْبِرِّ وَٱلتَّقْوَىٰ وَلَا تَعَاوَنُوا عَلَى ٱلْإِثْمِ وَٱلْعُدْوَٰنِ

Cooperate with one another in goodness and righteousness, and do not cooperate in sin and transgression. [5:2]

وَأَطِيعُوا ٱللَّهَ وَرَسُولَهُ وَلَا تَنَٰزَعُوا فَتَفْشَلُوا وَتَذْهَبَ رِيحُكُمْ وَٱصْبِرُوا إِنَّ ٱللَّهَ مَعَ ٱلصَّٰبِرِينَ ۝

Obey Allah and His Messenger and do not dispute with one another, or else you would falter and your dominance would dwindle. [8:46]

وَلَا تَكُونُوا كَٱلَّذِينَ تَفَرَّقُوا وَٱخْتَلَفُوا مِنۢ بَعْدِ مَا جَآءَهُمُ ٱلْبَيِّنَٰتُ وَأُوْلَٰٓئِكَ لَهُمْ عَذَابٌ عَظِيمٌ ۝

And do not be like those who split and differed after clear proofs had come to them. It is they who will suffer a tremendous punishment.
[3:105]

The Prophet ﷺ often spoke about the importance of remaining within the community. He said,

> Stay in the jama'ah, and beware of splitting, for Satan is with the one who is alone but farther from the pair. Whoever wants the summit of Paradise must then remain with the jama'ah.[5]

He also said, "*Whoever departs from the jama'ah by a handspan has removed the tie of Islam from his neck.*"[6]

In addition to warning against the dangers of splitting from the community, the Prophet ﷺ made a point to highlight the benefits of remaining within the community despite the difficulties. He said,

> The believer who interacts with the people and is patient with their harm has more reward than the believer who does not interact with people and is not patient with their harm.[7]

The Prophet ﷺ planted these values in the hearts of his Companions.

They valued the mission-driven community and saw it as indispensable to practicing Islam holistically and maintaining their high levels of commitment. Due to our individualistic and materialistic culture, we have veered significantly from valuing the collective in this way.

One of the early predecessors said, "The trouble of a community is better than the peace of mind of an individual." This spirit was embodied naturally by later generations following the Companions. Abdullab bin al-Mubarak, who was born about a century after the Prophet ﷺ passed away, writes that, "Were it not for the jamaʻah, we would never have gained any traction and the weak among us would be easy prey for the strong." Ibn al-Mubarak was highlighting the mission-driven community as the primary ingredient for the successful spread of Islam, and emphasized the ultimate goal of justice as a goal the jamaʻah must strive for.

FORGETTING DEATH AND THE AFTERLIFE

Forgetting the reality of death and the Afterlife can lead to a weakening of our will and motivation. When we are conscious of our looming death and entry into the next existence, our spirituality and commitment to Islam stays sharp and focused. In light of this, you can see the wisdom behind the Prophet's ﷺ instructions to visit graves after having prohibited it. He said to his Companions, *"I forbade you from visiting graves, but now visit them, for there is a lesson therein."*[8] In another wording he said, *"I once forbade you from visiting graves, but now visit graves, for doing so leads to better restraint in this life and reminds of the next."*[9]

We can also see clearly why he ﷺ was so keen on instructing his Companions to keep their own mortality in mind. Remembering death keeps the soul responsive and active. He addressed them one day and said, *"People! Be shy with Allah as He deserves to be!"* One man said, "Messenger of Allah, we are shy of Allah, the Exalted." He replied,

> Whoever among you is shy of Allah should not spend a single night wherein his death is not the first thing on his mind. He should safeguard his stomach and what it contains, his head and what it holds. He should remember death and the test of life, and he should leave off the glamour of this world.[10]

NEGLECTING DAILY WORSHIP

Neglecting one's individual duty to worship can also lead him or her to falter and burn out. Our daily worship regimen is designed to keep us on track spiritually, and if we are neglecting it, we should not be surprised when we lose momentum and feel demoralized. Some might sleep through Fajr prayer because they stayed up all night in unproductive conversations, or neglect to perform the sunnah prayers throughout the day. Some of us go days, weeks, or months without ever reciting or engaging with the Quran on a level beyond the audible. We might consider ourselves too busy (but in reality, too lazy) to perform proper *thikr* (remembrance) or go to the mosque for prayer. All of these choices and misaligned priorities have consequences that will manifest in our behavior and character.

The Prophet ﷺ indicated the dangers of failing to solidify an individual routine and commitment to worship. He said,

> Satan ties three knots on the nape of your neck when you sleep, sealing each knot saying, 'You have a long night, so sleep.' If you wake up and mention Allah, one knot is undone. If you make Wudu, another is undone. Then if you pray, the other is undone, and you arise energetic and good-spirited. Otherwise, you wake up disturbed within and lethargic.[11]

CONSUMING WHAT IS PROHIBITED OR UNETHICAL

When our vehicle runs on contaminated fuel, we may find ourselves stranded on the roadway. Similarly, fueling our bodies with impure sustenance will lead to lethargy in worship and good deeds.

You don't have to eat pork or drink alcohol to have something *haram* (prohibited) in your system. Many of us succumb to impure consumption simply by shortchanging or failing to perfect the daily work we get paid for, or indulging in dealings that fall into what we call the "grey area." These have subtle, destructive effects on our souls, and lead to our falling short in our worship and good deeds. Our prayer becomes a purely physical endeavor, and our *dua* (supplication) is void of the delightful feeling of being connected with our Creator.

Islam makes it clear that we must pay close attention to consuming what is permissible and avoiding anything with even the slightest doubt with regards to its permissibility. Notice in the following verse how Allah draws a connection between eating what is permissible and not following "Satan's footsteps," showing us clearly how being negligent of what we consume can eventually lead to more consequential sins:

يَـٰٓأَيُّهَا ٱلنَّاسُ كُلُوا۟ مِمَّا فِى ٱلْأَرْضِ حَلَـٰلًا طَيِّبًا وَلَا تَتَّبِعُوا۟ خُطُوَٰتِ ٱلشَّيْطَـٰنِ ۚ إِنَّهُۥ لَكُمْ عَدُوٌّ مُّبِينٌ ۝

O humanity! Eat from what is lawful and good on the earth and do not follow Satan's footsteps. He is truly your sworn enemy. [2:168]

Allah also ties eating what is good and lawful to being grateful to Him. We can deduce from this that choosing to eat what is impermissible or dubious is an act of ingratitude and a failure to thank Him for all of the good that He made available to us:

فَكُلُوا۟ مِمَّا رَزَقَكُمُ ٱللَّهُ حَلَـٰلًا طَيِّبًا وَٱشْكُرُوا۟ نِعْمَتَ ٱللَّهِ إِن كُنتُمْ إِيَّاهُ تَعْبُدُونَ ۝

So eat from the good, lawful things which Allah has provided for you, and be grateful for Allah's favors, if you worship Him. [16:114]

And then, out of His mercy and generosity, He reminds us that even if we think we can commit these crimes under the radar, without anyone around us ever knowing, He is intricately aware of what we do at all times.

يَـٰٓأَيُّهَا ٱلرُّسُلُ كُلُوا۟ مِنَ ٱلطَّيِّبَـٰتِ وَٱعْمَلُوا۟ صَـٰلِحًا ۖ إِنِّى بِمَا تَعْمَلُونَ عَلِيمٌ ۝
O messengers! Eat from what is good and lawful, and act righteously. Indeed, I fully know what you do. [23:51]

The Prophet ﷺ dedicated much of his time and energy to teaching us the importance of eating only what is good and pure. He said, *"The Hellfire is most entitled to every body that grows out of filth,"*[12] meaning that is sustained by what is impermissible. He also said,

> What is halal is clear, what is haram is clear, and between them are dubious matters. Whoever leaves off any sin that is dubious is even more cautious when it comes to what is clear. But whoever takes the risk with a sin that

is doubtful is likely to fall into what is clear. Sins are God's forbidden land, and whoever grazes alongside the forbidden land is likely to trespass into it.[13]

The Prophet ﷺ once said to his grandson, *"Leave off what gives you doubt for what does not give you doubt."*[14] And just as he cared to nurture and raise his own kin on this principle, Prophet Muhammad ﷺ taught the Muslims for generations thereafter by leading through example. He was hyperconscious of what he consumed, always opting on the side of caution. When he once found a date on the ground, he refused to eat it, saying, *"Had I not feared that it was designated for charity, I would have eaten it."*[15]

This example left a deep impact in the way Muslims operated, especially in the first generations. The early Muslim generations would thoroughly investigate everything they consumed and engaged in, practicing caution in what they ate, drank, wore, and even what they used as vehicles. If they found even the slightest reason to doubt the permissibility of something, they avoided it completely out of fear that it would lead them to committing sin and corrupting their hearts. They feared deprivation of good deeds and acceptance more than they feared deprivation of anything worldly. An example is this incident that Aishah narrated:

> Abu Bakr had a servant who used to bring him some food paid for from his earnings. One day, he brought something and Abu Bakr ate from it. The servant commented, "Do you know how I got the money for this?" Abu Bakr asked him to explain. The man said, "Once, in the pre-Islamic period, I foretold somebody's future though I did not know how to tell fortunes and cheated him. He gave me some money for that service and this is what you are eating from." Abu Bakr immediately forced himself to vomit, expelling all that he had consumed.[16]

FOCUSING ONLY ON ONE ASPECT OF RELIGION

Another cause of spiritual burnout is an imbalance in our understanding of Islam. Some students, teachers, and preachers make the mistake of giving their attention to only one out of the many sciences in our religion. They sacrifice even a basic understanding of other Islamic sciences for the one they feel is the most important.

Anyone who falls into this trap is inevitably bound to suffer spiritual burnout, for the dimensions of Islam complement each other. Islam is a religion that encompasses all facets of our life. Choosing to only take part in a portion of it is a flawed approach; it would be as if someone chose to only engage in one part of human life, neglecting the components that they dislike or don't care for. Thus it is natural that when one exhausts a single component of Islam, they feel as if there is no more work to be done, and so they either slow their pace or stop moving forward completely.

Allah's methodology is holistic. We learn this from the clear discourse of the Quran, wherein Allah teaches us to take Islam as a whole and not in parts:

يَٰٓأَيُّهَا ٱلَّذِينَ ءَامَنُوا۟ ٱدْخُلُوا۟ فِى ٱلسِّلْمِ كَآفَّةً وَلَا تَتَّبِعُوا۟ خُطُوَٰتِ ٱلشَّيْطَٰنِ إِنَّهُۥ لَكُمْ عَدُوٌّ مُّبِينٌ ۞

O believers! Enter into Islam wholeheartedly and do not follow Satan's footsteps. Surely he is your sworn enemy. [2:208]

To "*enter Islam wholeheartedly*" means to act upon all branches of our faith and pay mind to all of the duties of Islam. Allah then warns us against following Satan, who is working hard to divert you from this wholesome and holistic approach to God's religion. Satan knows that driving a person to delve deeply into one aspect of Islamic practice at the expense of the others will eventually lead them to lose momentum.

IGNORING ALLAH'S PATTERNS AND DIVINE WAYS

We often see a group among those who work for Islam who aim to change society as a whole. They hope to uproot everything around them, including people's thoughts, emotions, traditions, behaviors, and social structures. Their objectives span every level of existence, from local to political to economic, and they expect it all to happen overnight. Even their approach is idealistic and grandiose, lacking any element of practicality. This naive and erroneous approach can quickly lead to frustration and burnout.

Even though the intention may be righteous, such individuals fail to use the tools that Allah gave us, with which we are expected to operate in the world. They do not take into account the patterns and constants upon which Allah structures our lives and environments, such as the importance of gradual growth, the necessity of patience and purification, and the reality that victory ultimately returns to those who are most conscious of Allah, not the most worldly and vocal. They overlook the temporality of everything in this world. No one can edit Allah's timeline. When they eventually experience the gritty reality and realize that things were not as they had dreamed, those who took an unrealistic approach to their work become discouraged and reach a standstill in their work.

PHYSICAL EXHAUSTION

Some people exert all of the time and energy they have into serving this religion, withholding from themselves any comfort and relief. This is understandable, for there is so much work to be done with so few who are working for these causes. But these generous, sacrificing souls must be cautious against taking on unsustainable amounts of work and pressure, leading to their eventual physical and spiritual burnout.

The Prophet ﷺ heavily emphasized the right of our bodies over us. His message and example was one of balance and moderation, and he made a point to remind the Companions of their priorities. He said, *"Your Lord has a right over you, your self has a right over you, and your family has a right over you, so give each their due right."*[17] In another narration he said, *"Your body has a right over you, your eyes have a right over you, your spouse has a right over you, and your guests have a right over you."*[18]

LACK OF PREPARATION FOR CHALLENGES

Many of us start this journey of Islamic work without even considering some of the challenges that might arise. These challenges can come from our spouses, our children, the world's glamour, or a divine test of our patience during hardship. If we hit these speed bumps in our journeys without taking the proper caution to look out for them and brace for their impact, we may be unable to get past them. This could be the source of our spiritual burnout, slacking on our duties, and giving up.

Allah calls our attention to the urgent need to prepare ourselves for obstacles like this all throughout the Quran. Allah guarantees that we will encounter dangers along the road so that we can prepare for them:

مَّا كَانَ ٱللَّهُ لِيَذَرَ ٱلْمُؤْمِنِينَ عَلَىٰ مَآ أَنتُمْ عَلَيْهِ حَتَّىٰ يَمِيزَ ٱلْخَبِيثَ مِنَ ٱلطَّيِّبِ

Allah would not leave the believers in the condition you were in,
until He distinguished the good from the evil... [3:179]

The most common, and arguably most painful, challenges come from within our own home. God says,

يَـٰٓأَيُّهَا ٱلَّذِينَ ءَامَنُوٓاْ إِنَّ مِنْ أَزْوَٰجِكُمْ وَأَوْلَٰدِكُمْ عَدُوًّا لَّكُمْ فَٱحْذَرُوهُمْ ۚ
وَإِن تَعْفُواْ وَتَصْفَحُواْ وَتَغْفِرُواْ فَإِنَّ ٱللَّهَ غَفُورٌ رَّحِيمٌ ۝ إِنَّمَآ أَمْوَٰلُكُمْ
وَأَوْلَٰدُكُمْ فِتْنَةٌ ۚ وَٱللَّهُ عِندَهُۥٓ أَجْرٌ عَظِيمٌ ۝

O believers! Indeed, some of your spouses and children are enemies
to you, so beware of them. But if you pardon, overlook, and forgive,
then Allah is truly All-Forgiving, Most Merciful. Your wealth and
children are only a test, but Allah has a great reward. [64:14-15]

And in another verse,

وَٱعْلَمُوٓاْ أَنَّمَآ أَمْوَٰلُكُمْ وَأَوْلَٰدُكُمْ فِتْنَةٌ وَأَنَّ ٱللَّهَ عِندَهُۥٓ أَجْرٌ عَظِيمٌ ۝

And know that your wealth and your children are only a test and
that with Allah is a great reward. [8:28]

Allah described some of our closest family members as enemies because they may distract us from our goal; their proximity to us is what is most threatening to our success. But our Lord points out that just as this enemy comes from whom we would least suspect, we must employ unconventional tactics in our defense: pardon, tolerance, and forgiveness. He then emphasized the "great reward" in store for those who make it through the tests of family without having turned back, resorted to ill character, or given up their pursuit of Allah's pleasure.

These challenges will be present on the road for as long as we trek it. Neither our claim to be believers nor our righteous actions can secure us from encountering these tests. God says,

الٓمٓ ۝ أَحَسِبَ ٱلنَّاسُ أَن يُتْرَكُوٓاْ أَن يَقُولُوٓاْ ءَامَنَّا وَهُمْ لَا يُفْتَنُونَ ۝
وَلَقَدْ فَتَنَّا ٱلَّذِينَ مِن قَبْلِهِمْ فَلَيَعْلَمَنَّ ٱللَّهُ ٱلَّذِينَ صَدَقُواْ وَلَيَعْلَمَنَّ
ٱلْكَٰذِبِينَ ۝

*Alif-Lām-Mīm. Do people think once they say, "We believe," that
they will be left without being put to the test? We certainly tested
those before them. And Allah will clearly distinguish between those
who are truthful and those who are liars.* [29:1-3]

Allah also says:

وَلَنَبْلُوَنَّكُمْ حَتَّىٰ نَعْلَمَ ٱلْمُجَٰهِدِينَ مِنكُمْ وَٱلصَّٰبِرِينَ وَنَبْلُوَاْ أَخْبَارَكُمْ ۝

*We will certainly test you until We prove those of you who struggle
and remain steadfast, and reveal how you conduct yourselves.* [47:31]

FRIENDS WHO DRAG YOU DOWN

Those who are engaged in Islamic work might find themselves
engaging with influencers and celebrities in the community. After
seeing these figures up close and witnessing how they operate behind
the scenes, the Islamic worker may discover that in some cases these
celebrities are borderline charlatans who are able to maintain an
appealing shell without much substance. This realization can lead to
frustration and a negative, dispirited outlook that can spread like a
plague, deterring the once-inspired worker from trusting anyone or
putting any real work into their own development. If all you need is
a microphone or a platform to gain a following in religious circles,
Satan may convince you to take shortcuts in your spirituality and
self-development for the sake of keeping up with a certain trend.

This is why the Prophet ﷺ repeatedly drew our attention to the
importance of the quality of the company we keep. He said, *"A
person is upon the religion of his closest friend, so look at who
you take as a close friend."*[19] He also compared the good friend to
a perfume seller who, *"will either offer you some free of charge, or
you will buy some from him, or you will smell from him a pleasant
fragrance."* Then he compared a bad friend to a blacksmith, who,
*"either will burn your clothing, or you will smell a foul smell from
him."*[20]

LACK OF ORGANIZED PRIORITIES

Many Islamic workers lack any structure to their approach to God's religion. They don't follow any particular program or develop an organized approach to their goals, self-improvement, and Islamic work. Such disorder results in a misalignment of priorities and scattered focus and efforts. It can also be the result of lack of training and education about the proper ordering of things.

Haphazard priorities may lead someone to spend most of their time on something that has little to no importance, thereby neglecting the foundational components of Islam. It is a plan for disaster, as every wasted moment only delays their arrival and adds to their burdens. And unless God intervenes for their benefit, they will find themselves slackening and losing the momentum they initially began with.

In light of this, we can understand the Prophet's ﷺ parting advice to his dear friend Muadh ibn Jabal as the latter was leaving to go teach the new Muslims of Yemen. Muadh was still young at the time, and though he had a deep understanding of the religion, the Prophet ﷺ emphasized to him the importance of establishing priorities. He said to him,

> You are going to a group from the People of the Scripture. Call them to testify that there is nothing worthy of worship but Allah, and that I am the Messenger of Allah. If they comply with that, teach them that Allah obligated them with charity that is taken from their rich and redistributed among their poor. If they comply with that, then avoid their most prized properties, and beware of the prayer of the oppressed, for there is no veil between it and Allah.[21]

The prescriptions in this hadith regarding priorities are essential when assessing and developing our approach to Islamic work.

BELITTLING THE EFFECTS OF SMALL SINS

When we begin to falter and slow down, we must consider that it might be due to the heavy pile of sins on our backs. Allah would never slow us down from reaching Him without a just reason, and it might very well be the sins we brushed off as trivial that come together to form the glass ceiling that limits our ascension. Allah says,

$$\text{وَمَآ أَصَـٰبَكُم مِّن مُّصِيبَةٍ فَبِمَا كَسَبَتْ أَيْدِيكُمْ وَيَعْفُواْ عَن كَثِيرٍ ۝}$$

*Whatever affliction befalls you is because of what your own hands
have committed. And He pardons much.* [42:30]

The Messenger of Allah ﷺ also draws our attention to the destructive potential of seemingly small sins, reminding us to take great caution to avoid them. He said, *"Beware of the sins that are belittled, for they will certainly gather over someone until they destroy him."* Then he drew a comparison to put it into perspective:

> It is just like when a group camps out in an open ground. When it is time to eat, one man goes off and brings back one branch, another man brings another branch, all until they gather a large pile and light a fire, scorching whatever they throw therein.[22]

The Prophet ﷺ also warned against the scarring effect of sins on our hearts. He said,

> When a believer commits a sin, he stains his heart with a black dot. If he repents, desists, and asks for forgiveness, his heart is polished, but if he continues, it increases until it overtakes his heart. That is the stain that He, Mighty and Majestic, mentions in the Quran...

and then he recited,[23]

$$\text{كَلَّا ۖ بَلْ ۜ رَانَ عَلَىٰ قُلُوبِهِم مَّا كَانُواْ يَكْسِبُونَ ۝}$$

*But no! In fact, their hearts have been stained by what they used to
commit!* [83:14]

EXCESSIVENESS IN WORSHIP

Occupying oneself in unbalanced worship while depriving the body of its due right of relief and comfort leads to fatigue and burnout, and even turning toward a different, or possibly opposite, direction. Someone who begins their journey overzealously will eventually become apathetic and negligent if they do not correct their approach. This consequence is only natural, as our capacities are limited, and once they are exceeded, we will shut down.

Islam advocates balance and prohibits excessiveness in all matters. The Prophet ﷺ said, *"Beware of excessiveness in matters of worship, for those before you only perished due to excessiveness in worship.*"[24] He ﷺ also said, *"The zealots are doomed!"* and repeated it three times.[25] The Prophet ﷺ clearly warned against being too hard on ourselves when he said, *"Do not be too intense on yourselves, for you will then be dealt with harshly. One group of people were intense on themselves, and they were dealt with harshly, and here they remain in the monasteries and temples."* Then he cited the verse from the Quran:[26]

وَرَهْبَانِيَّةً ابْتَدَعُوهَا مَا كَتَبْنَاهَا عَلَيْهِمْ

As for monasticism, they made it up—We never ordained it for them... [57:27]

The Prophet ﷺ also said, *"This religion is ease. Anyone who makes the religion harsh will be defeated."*[27]

Anas bin Mālik, who served as the Prophet's assistant for a decade, narrates that three men came to the wives of the Prophet ﷺ to ask about how he worshipped in private. When they left, they reasoned that they should perform even more worship than the Prophet ﷺ in order to compensate for their lesser status. They reasoned, "Where are we compared to the Prophet ﷺ? All of his sins have already been forgiven!" One of them declared that he would pray all night without sleeping, another that he would fast every day, and the third that he would abstain from marriage. When the Messenger of Allah ﷺ heard this, he approached them and said,

> Are you the ones who said this and that? By God, I am the most fearful of God among you and the most cognizant of Him, but I fast some days and eat others, I pray and I sleep, and I marry women. So whoever is averse to my path is not associated with me.[28]

Aishah narrates that the Prophet ﷺ once came home while there was another woman present with her. He asked, *"Who was she?"* Aishah replied, "She is a woman who is praised for her [nonstop] prayers." He disapproved, saying,

> No. Take on what you can handle. By Allah, Allah does not stop rewarding until you stop doing good deeds, and the most beloved religious commitment to Him is one that a person remains consistent upon.[29]

The Prophet 🌿 also said, *"Only take on deeds that you can handle. Allah does not waiver until you waiver, and the most beloved deeds to Allah are the most consistent, even if small."*[30]

Ibn Abbas narrates that one of the Prophet's female servants used to fast every day and pray all night. The Prophet was told that she would do this, and so he said,

> Every action has a high time, and the high point leads to a slump. Whoever's slump is according to my sunnah has followed the right guidance, and whoever's slump is according to anything else has gone astray.[31]

Effects on Individual & Community

Spiritual burnout has harmful and destructive effects on both the volunteers working for Islam and on their community work. As with all of the roadblocks covered in this book, the effect of individuals succombing to a spiritual disease has repercussions for the entire community, slowing our progress as a whole.

On the individual level, the roadblock of spiritual burnout jeopardizes the very destiny of those who fall victim to it by causing them to accumulate fewer deeds. One might even pass away while in this state of apathy, having once been active and motivated but finally meeting Allah in a state of negligence.

This is why the Messenger of Allah 🌿 used to actively seek Allah's help from laziness and incompetence. He would pray,

> Allah, I seek refuge in You from worry and grief, from incompetence and laziness, from cowardice and stinginess, and from being overwhelmed by debt and overpowered by men.[32]

He would also say, *"Allah, make the best of my life the last of it, the best of my deeds the last of them, and the best of my days the day I meet You."*[33] One of his statements of encouragement to his nation was: *"When Allah wants good for someone, He uses them."* Someone asked, "How does He use them, Messenger of Allah?" He said, *"He grants them success with a good deed before death."*[34]

He 🌿 also said,

> Someone may do the deeds of the people of the Hellfire, while he is actually one of the people of Paradise; and he

might do the deeds of the people of Paradise, while he is actually one of the people of the Hellfire. Deeds are determined by their endings.[35]

The Prophet also advised, *"Do not be impressed by anyone until you look to see what ending is given to him."*[36]

The Prophet's ﷺ heavy emphasis on life's ending affected the Companions deeply, especially Abdullah bin Mas'ood. When Abdullah fell ill and sensed that he was nearing death, he wept. He said to the people around him, *"I only weep because death came to me in a time when I am in a state of rest, not in a state of hard work."*[37] What he meant was that this fatal illness caught him at a time of decreased worship and activity relative to the rest of his life.

Spiritual burnout also has effects on the community as a whole and the trajectory of collective Islamic work. It makes the road longer and the tasks harder for everyone, not just for the individual whose commitment has lagged. There are fewer people to carry the work, and those few are more vulnerable amidst a pessimistic and apathetic community culture. According to God's tradition, victory is not given to the lazy or to those who give up. It is reserved for those who put in the work and perfect their efforts. Allah says,

إِنَّ ٱلَّذِينَ ءَامَنُواْ وَعَمِلُواْ ٱلصَّٰلِحَٰتِ إِنَّا لَا نُضِيعُ أَجْرَ مَنْ أَحْسَنَ عَمَلًا ۝

As for those who believe and do good, We certainly never deny the reward of those who are best in deeds. [18:30]

وَٱلَّذِينَ جَٰهَدُواْ فِينَا لَنَهْدِيَنَّهُمْ سُبُلَنَا ۚ وَإِنَّ ٱللَّهَ لَمَعَ ٱلْمُحْسِنِينَ ۝

As for those who struggle in Our cause, We will surely guide them along Our Way. And Allah is certainly with the good-doers. [29:69]

Remedies of Spiritual Burnout

Considering the great dangers that the roadblock of spiritual burnout leads to, we must learn how to immunize ourselves against it and treat it when it overtakes us. This can be done in a number of ways:

1. Keeping a safe distance from all types of sins
Sins are like a fire that incinerates our hearts. They earn us God's anger, which is the ultimate loss one can experience. Allah says,

وَمَن يَحْلِلْ عَلَيْهِ غَضَبِي فَقَدْ هَوَىٰ ۞

And whoever My wrath befalls is certainly doomed. [20:81]

2. Consistency in our daily routines

A daily routine of *thikr* (remembrance), *dua* (supplication), reciting Quran, and sunnah prayers is what sustains a healthy level of faith in the heart. It keeps our souls nourished and energized, our motivations high and our ambitions focused. Allah says,

وَهُوَ ٱلَّذِى جَعَلَ ٱلَّيْلَ وَٱلنَّهَارَ خِلْفَةً لِّمَنْ أَرَادَ أَن يَذَّكَّرَ أَوْ أَرَادَ شُكُورًا ۞

And He is the One Who causes the day and the night to alternate for whoever desires to be mindful or to be grateful. [25:62]

He directs us to use the alternation of time and the world around us as a means to remember Him, to ensure that we don't let a single day or night pass without giving our souls the attention and sustenance needed to carry on. Consider also one of the first ayahs that God revealed to the Prophet ﷺ. Shortly after having received the mantle of prophethood, the Prophet ﷺ began to worry about his own ability to carry out this task with its due right. He fled home after an encounter with the angel Gabriel and buried himself in a garment out of fear from the responsibility that awaited him. Then God sent down:

يَـٰٓأَيُّهَا ٱلْمُزَّمِّلُ ۞ قُمِ ٱلَّيْلَ إِلَّا قَلِيلًا ۞ نِّصْفَهُ أَوِ ٱنقُصْ مِنْهُ قَلِيلًا ۞ أَوْ
زِدْ عَلَيْهِ وَرَتِّلِ ٱلْقُرْءَانَ تَرْتِيلًا ۞ إِنَّا سَنُلْقِى عَلَيْكَ قَوْلًا ثَقِيلًا ۞

*O you wrapped in a garment! Stand all night except a little—
half the night, or a little less, or a little more—and recite the
Quran in a measured way. We will soon send upon you a
weighty revelation.* [73:1-5]

Allah acknowledged the ponderous task of receiving the revelation from the Lord of all Creation and relaying it to all of mankind for generations to come. He knew that attempting such an ambitious task without proper nourishment of the self could be destructive to the Messenger and the message itself. And so He commanded our beloved Prophet ﷺ with two simple solutions: stand in prayer at night and recite the Quran with deliberate reflection.

Not only did the Prophet ﷺ keep his own worship sustainably consistent, but he also urged the rest of us to always be keen on maintaining our worship routines. He instructed regarding our nightly recitation of Quran, *"Whoever sleeps past his usual routine or part of it and then recites it between the Fajr and Zuhr prayers, then it is recorded for him as if he recited it during the night."*[38]

3. Taking advantage of blessed times

Paying attention to the time of day, month, or year, and connecting them to the various virtues that God embedded within them is an excellent way to reenergize our souls and recharge our wills. The Prophet ﷺ said, *"Aim straight, come close, rejoice, and seek strength [through worship] in the morning, the evening, and during a part of the night."*[39]

4. Liberating ourselves of religious excessiveness

Shedding any extreme or excessive religious tendencies helps us keep our worship sustainable. Aishah narrates that the Prophet ﷺ had a straw mat that he would use as his niche to pray in during the night, when people would come to pray with him, and he would spread it out during the day. The people crowded around him one night, so he said, *"People, you must only take on deeds that you can handle, for Allah does not stop rewarding until you stop doing good deeds. The most beloved deeds to Allah are those that are done consistently, even if they are small."* When Muhammad's family did an action, they would remain firm upon it.[40]

It is necessary to point out here that avoiding excessiveness does not mean to be negligent and lazy. Rather we must be moderate and balanced, maintaining the actions we are used to doing and striving to follow the Prophet's example. Abdullah bin 'Amr bin al-As narrates that the Messenger of Allah ﷺ once told him, *"Abdullah, do not be like that man. He used to pray all night, and now he does not pray at all at night."*[41] Abu Hurayrah narrates that the Messenger of Allah ﷺ said, *"When I forbid you from something, avoid it completely, and when I instruct you with something, do as much of it as you can."*[42]

5. Joining the community and collective work

Knowing very well the dangerous risks of isolation, and a tendency of people to mistake seclusion for pious restraint, the Messenger of Allah 🙷 heavily emphasized the importance of the community to his Companions. He said, *"The community is a mercy, and division is torment."*[43] He also said, *"Allah's hand is with the jama'ah."*[44] Ali bin Abu Talib, who proved his deep understanding of this concept by bravely putting his life on the line for the unity of the Muslims decades after the Prophet's 🙷 death, said, "The trouble of a community is better than the peace of mind of an individual."

6. Paying close attention to God's divine laws and patterns

Allah says,

فَلَن تَجِدَ لِسُنَّتِ ٱللَّهِ تَبْدِيلًا ۖ وَلَن تَجِدَ لِسُنَّتِ ٱللَّهِ تَحْوِيلًا ۝

You will find no change in the way of Allah, nor will you find it diverted. [35:43]

We must understand Allah's divine ways and patterns with human beings and the world—they include unchangeable laws such as gradual change and the necessity of effort and doing one's best. Allah says,

ذَٰلِكَ وَلَوْ يَشَآءُ ٱللَّهُ لَٱنتَصَرَ مِنْهُمْ وَلَٰكِن لِّيَبْلُوَا۟ بَعْضَكُم بِبَعْضٍ

So will it be. Had Allah willed, He could have inflicted punishment on them. But He tests some of you by means of others. [47:4]

When reflecting over the constants in God's creation, we should understand that meaningful change occurs gradually out of the mercy of Allah. Aishah pointed out that the first revelations to come down were concise surahs that mentioned Paradise and the Hellfire. Then when people flocked to Islam, the rulings of permissible and prohibited came down. She said, "If the first thing to come down was, 'Do not drink wine,' they would have said, 'We will never abandon wine!' And if it was, 'Do not fornicate,' they would have said, 'We will never stop fornicating!'"[45] Here Aishah was pointing out the divine wisdom in the gradual unveiling of Islamic obligations.

Umar bin Abdul-Aziz, who was the first caliph to revive justice and righteousness after the demise of the Companions, had a son named Abdul-Malik who was full of youthful courage and energy. He would often criticize his father for being too slow in eradicating the remnants of injustice from the previous rulers. He once said to his father, "Why is it that you do not solve matters immediately? By Allah, I do not care if they burn us at the stake for the truth!" His wise father responded, "Do not rush, my son. Allah dispraised wine twice in the Quran before finally declaring it prohibited. I fear that if I enforce the truth onto the people all at once, they will leave it all at once, and chaos would ensue."[46]

7. Anticipating the obstacles beforehand

Learning about what our path has in store for us from those who have already trekked some distance in Islamic work helps us stay prepared and ready to encounter the inevitable obstacles. It also ensures that we have the tools and knowledge necessary for overcoming them. This leaves no room for us to unwittingly fall into frustration and burnout.

8. Being consistent and methodical in our work

We must check to make sure that the most pressing matter is first on our list, and that we are not spending time and effort in secondary and marginal issues. Our battles are to be chosen carefully. We should have solid habits and mechanisms in place for our workflow, protecting us from any sudden waves of lethargy, and preventing us from being sidetracked by things that are of minor significance.

9. Spending time with hardworking, righteous people

Be keen on spending time with righteous Muslims who are focused on serving and pleasing Allah. They have pure souls, glowing hearts, and enlightened spirits that attract and energize the drive and ambition of anyone in their company. Their unwavering sense of purpose fuels our will to continue on the path with our destination in mind. The Prophet ﷺ drew our attention to this when he once asked his Companions, *"May I tell you who is the best of the people?"* Eagerly they responded, "Yes, Messenger of Allah!" He said, *"One who reminds you of Allah, Mighty and Majestic, when you look at him."*[47]

23

10. *Giving our bodies their due right of sleep, food, and drink*

We must be carefully balanced in our approach to comfort and consumption. They can be means of replenishing our physical energy, strength, and vitality if taken in moderation, but can lead to a physical and spiritual destruction if we allow ourselves to indulge thoughtlessly. Our approach must be in accordance with the daily call of the angels: "What is little, but sufficient, is better than what is plenty, but diverting."[48]

The Messenger of Allah ﷺ taught us this sense of balance, not only in his exemplary way of life, but also in how he instructed his companions. He once walked into the mosque and saw a string extending between two pillars. He asked, *"What is this rope?"* They said, "This is Zaynab's rope. When she gets fatigued, she uses it to hold herself upright." The Prophet ﷺ said, *"Untie it. You must pray with your energy, and when you grow tired, then rest."*[49] He also said,

> When any of you grows sleepy as he is praying he should sleep in order to rid himself of drowsiness. If someone prays while he is sleepy, he does not know—perhaps he may intend to ask for forgiveness but instead curse himself.[50]

11. *Relaxing the soul with healthy amusements*

There is a lot that Allah permitted for us to find pleasure and delight in. It starts within our very own home—which we should strive to make a space for comfort and security rather than tension and gloom. We must give ourselves time to play with our children and spend quality time with our spouses, and even take trips and vacations that are within our means. We can spend a day in the wilderness, engaging in recreation or quiet contemplation while exploring nature and reflecting upon God's creation as a family. We can take hikes together, practicing cooperation and teamwork by traveling at a pace suitable for all and encouraging one another to keep climbing even when it seems unbearable. Marveling at the glorious view and remembering Allah's beauty through it when you finally reach the end of the trail is an experience that will reenergize your soul and renew your motivation to continue on with your work for Islam.

Hanzalah bin al-Rabee', who was one of the Prophet's ﷺ scribes, once met Abu Bakr on the road. He asked, "How are you, Hanzalah?"

He replied, "Hanzalah is a hypocrite!" shamefully referring to himself in the third person. Abu Bakr said, "Subḥān Allah! What are you saying?!" He explained, "When we are with the Messenger of Allah ﷺ, he reminds us of Paradise and the Hellfire, and it is as if we can see it with our own eyes. Then when we leave the Messenger of Allah ﷺ, we have fun with our wives and children and businesses, and we forget so much." Abu Bakr said, "By Allah, I experience the same thing." They then went to the Messenger of Allah ﷺ and said to him, "Hanzalah is a hypocrite!" When the Messenger of Allah ﷺ asked why he said that, he responded with the same, "Messenger of Allah, when we are with you, you remind us of the Hellfire and Paradise until it is as if we can see it with our own eyes. Then when we leave you, we enjoy our time with our wives, children, and businesses, and we forget so much." The Messenger of Allah ﷺ responded,

> I swear by the One in whose hand is my soul, if you were to always be upon what you are when you are with me—in a state of remembrance—the Angels would shake your hands on your very beds and in the streets. Rather, Hanzalah it is one moment at a time.

He repeated that last phrase three times.[51]

12. Reading and reflecting on the life story of the Prophet ﷺ

The Prophet's biography is filled with many lessons and practical models for Islamic work. He and his Companions were the epitome of hard work, high ambitions, unwavering commitment, and pure intentions. Reading their stories revitalizes our souls and generates within us a love for emulating their examples. This is why Allah says about the stories of the prophets:

$$لَقَدْ كَانَ فِى قَصَصِهِمْ عِبْرَةٌ لِّأُوْلِى ٱلْأَلْبَٰبِ$$

In their stories there is truly a lesson for people of reason. [12:111]

We can also find these examples in the lives of the scholars and righteous men and women who lived after the Prophet's time. Umar bin Abdul-Aziz, for example, used to dedicate the time from the end of the Fajr prayer until shortly after sunrise to remembering Allah. Whenever he would feel tired or fatigued, he would walk laps around the courtyard of his house repeating a verse of poetry:

How can I afford any rest for my eye
When I don't know where I will be

Our spirits and emotions should be shaken when we catch a glimpse of these snapshots from the lives of these heroes. We draw from their will and fortitude the motivation we need to continue on in our journey of Islamic work.

13. Remembering death

Reflecting on death, the time in our graves, and the everlasting paradise or punishment wakes our souls from slumber and startles us into a state of awareness. It gives us the nudge that we often need to continue our march towards Allah. The best way to remember death is to visit the graveyards, even just once a week. There we can learn many lessons by reflecting on the many who once had great health, beautiful families, and so many hopes and dreams, whose bodies now lie under the soil deteriorating slowly. This is why the Messenger of Allah ﷺ said, *"I once forbade you from visiting the graveyards, but now visit them, for there is a lesson therein."*[52]

A tenth-century scholar named Ibn al-Sammāk dug a ditch in his house that looked like a grave. Whenever he felt himself slacking off or being lazy, he would go into that ditch and imagine himself dead. He would picture the questioning of the angels, remember his shortcomings, and begin to shout the plea described in the Quran:

$$رَبِّ ٱرْجِعُونِ ۞ لَعَلِّيٓ أَعْمَلُ صَٰلِحًا فِيمَا تَرَكْتُ$$

"My Lord! Let me go back, so I may do good in what I left behind." [23:99]

After all of this, he would say to himself, "Ibn Sammāk, you've been given another chance!" and then get out of the grave as if he was born anew.

14. Remembering Paradise and the Hellfire

The sheer thought of permanent pleasures and pains of the afterlife should be enough to stir our spirits and spark the sense of urgency and drive that we need when our commitment starts to wane. Harim ibn Hayyan, a pious man who worked for Umar ibn al-Khattab, was known to go out of his house on some nights to call out at the top of his lungs, "How can anyone who seeks Paradise sleep!? How can anyone who fears the Hellfire sleep?!" Then he would recite the ayah,[53]

$$أَفَأَمِنَ أَهْلُ ٱلْقُرَىٰ أَن يَأْتِيَهُم بَأْسُنَا بَيَـٰتًا وَهُمْ نَآئِمُونَ ۝$$

Did the people of those societies feel secure that Our punishment would not come upon them by night while they were asleep? [7:97]

15. Attending gatherings of knowledge

Knowledge restores life to the hearts. Who can know what sincere word from a truthful scholar might motivate us for an entire year, or possibly for our whole life? Those short moments in which our hearts absorb such impactful words can give us the energy we need to sustain our work for years.

The transformational potential of knowledge is no secret to anyone who reflects on the Quran. Allah says,

$$إِنَّمَا يَخْشَى ٱللَّهَ مِنْ عِبَادِهِ ٱلْعُلَمَـٰٓؤُا۟$$

It is only the knowledgeable who fear Allah from among His servants. [35:28]

He even directed the Prophet ﷺ to say,

$$رَّبِّ زِدْنِي عِلْمًا ۝$$

"My Lord! Increase me in knowledge." [20:114]

16. Taking a comprehensive approach to religion

Often out of zeal, excitement, and passion, many who begin Islamic work direct their focus on one facet of Islam. This is an impossible impediment to spiritual advancement and sustainability. Approaching Islam as the all-encompassing way of life that God intended it to be ensures that our direction stays straight and our pace stays steady until we meet Allah.

17. Constant self-assessment

Keeping track of ourselves and examining our own progress is a pro-active and preventative way to avoid getting caught in any traps on our journey. We must set standards for ourselves and hold ourselves accountable to them, rewarding ourselves for compliance and setting consequences for ourselves for veering off track. Allah teaches us to assess ourselves and what we have prepared for our own futures:

$$يَٰٓأَيُّهَا ٱلَّذِينَ ءَامَنُوا۟ ٱتَّقُوا۟ ٱللَّهَ وَلْتَنظُرْ نَفْسٌ مَّا قَدَّمَتْ لِغَدٍۖ وَٱتَّقُوا۟ ٱللَّهَۚ إِنَّ ٱللَّهَ خَبِيرٌۢ بِمَا تَعْمَلُونَ ۝$$

O believers! Be mindful of Allah and let every soul look to what it has sent forth for tomorrow. And fear Allah—certainly Allah is All-Aware of what you do. [59:18]

✦ ✦ ✦ ✦

ENDNOTES

1. Al-Sābooni, Safwat al-Tafāseer, vol. 2, pp. 257, 258
2. al-Tirmidhi, #2380
3. al-Mundhiri, al-Targheeb wal-Tarheeb, v. 3, p. 137
4. al-Hindi, Kanz al-'Ummāl, #6309
5. al-Tirmidhi, #2165
6. al-Tirmidhi, #2863
7. al-Tirmidhi, #2507
8. Ahmad, v. 3, p. 38
9. al-Tirmidhi, #1054
10. al-Tirmidhi, #2458
11. al-Bukhari, v. 2, p. 65; Muslim, #776
12. al-Isfahāni, Hilyah al-Awliyā', v. 1, p. 31
13. al-Bukhari, v. 3, p. 70; Muslim #1599
14. al-Tirmidhi, #2518
15. al-Bukhari, v. 3, p. 71; Muslim, #1071
16. al-Bukhari, v. 5, p. 53
17. al-Bukhari, v. 3, p. 49
18. al-Bukhari, v. 3, p. 51
19. al-Tirmidhi, #2378
20. al-Bukhari, v. 3, p. 82; Muslim, #2628
21. al-Bukhari, v. 2, pp. 108, 109; Muslim, #19
22. Ahmad, v. 1, p. 402
23. Ibn Majah #4244
24. Ahmad, al-Musnad, v. 1, p. 215
25. Muslim, #2670
26. Abu Dawud, #4904
27. al-Bukhari, v. 1, p. 16
28. al-Bukhari, v. 7, p. 2 (in this wording); Muslim, v. 2, p. 1020
29. al-Bukhari, v. 1, p. 17 (in this wording; Muslim, #782
30. al-Bukhari, v. 3, p. 49; and Muslim, #1103
31. al-Haythami, Majma' al-Zawā'id, v. 2, pp. 261, 262
32. Abu Dawud, #1540
33. al-Haythami, Majma' al-Zawā'id, v 10, pp. 160, 161
34. al-Tirmidhi, #2142
35. al-Bukhari, v. 8, p. 155
36. Ahmad, v. 3, p. 120
37. Ibn al-Atheer, v. 3 p. 408
38. Muslim, #747
39. al-Bukhari, v. 1, p. 16
40. Muslim, 782
41. al-Bukhari, v. 2, p. 68; Muslim #1159
42. al-Bukhari, v. 9, p. 118; Muslim, 1337
43. Ahmad, v. 4, p. 278, 375

44. al-Tirmidhi, #2166
45. al-Bukhari, v. 6, p. 228
46. al-Shātibi, al-Muwāfaqāt, v. 2, p. 94
47. Ahmad, v 6, p. 459
48. al-Hākim, al-Mustadrak, #1431
49. al-Bukhari, v. 2, p. 67; Muslim, #784
50. al-Bukhari, v. 1, p. 63, 64; Muslim, #786
51. Muslim, #2750
52. Ahmad, v. 3, p. 38
53. al-Isfahani, Hilyat al-Awliya, v. 2, p. 119

Extravagance

In our times of excess and consumption, the roadblock of extravagance and over-indulgence is a widespread affliction among Islamic workers. This roadblock slows our progress, erodes our efforts, dulls our spirituality, and steals away our time and energy. Since this phenomenon comes in many forms, and is a distinct quality of our culture and era, it is important to clarify what we mean by extravagance.

Linguistically, *isrāf* refers to a wasteful squandering of resources. It also refers to defiantly transgressing boundaries. So when we use this word in reference to those who work for Islam, we intend by it overstepping one's limits of moderation. It can refer to consumption of food and drink, clothing, entertainment, and any other human inclination to luxury and comfort. It can also include being overly distracted by material possessions, upgrades, online shopping, and appearing fashionable. We used the term extravagance as a translation for *isrāf*, although over-indulgence and excessive spending are also apt translations.

You may have succumbed to extravagance and over-indulgence if:

- ✓ You find it difficult to perform basic acts of worship, especially fasting and waking up for prayer.
- ✓ You are easily distracted from your goals
- ✓ You spend much less in charity, proportionately, than you used to.
- ✓ You rarely deny yourself any desired pleasure or comfort.

✓ You never have enough and are always looking to increase what you have.

✓ You are always thinking about worldly delights, collecting them, looking at them, planning for them, and talking about them.

✓ You don't feel any blessings or *barakah* in your wealth or time.

> "Many years ago I was a student making a fraction of my current income. I budgeted before buying anything, and many things were unnecessary because I couldn't afford them. Life was simple with many blessings, and we were busy contributing to dawah, and Allah blessed the efforts.
>
> Fast forward to now—we live a life of excess. Whatever food we desire is delivered to our door with the click of a button. We even find good intentions for it, but rarely do we seek intentions abstaining from it. We vacation anywhere we like, ride the latest cars, and dress in brand names. We grew busy enjoying worldly pleasures, and it reflected on our effort and attention, and maybe even the time we give supplicating for our dawah work. Gradually this world moved from our hands to our hearts and it reflected on our actions. Until we regularly evaluate, remember death, and surround ourselves with the right company, we will fall short of the mark."

Causes of Extravagance

Extravagance can arise in even the most Islamic environments for a number of reasons.

- Upbringing
- Wealth after poverty
- Extravagant friends
- Neglecting to prepare for journey
- Family pressures
- Misunderstanding the nature of life
- Weak willpower
- Ignoring the severity of the Day of Resurrection
- Forgetting the realities of human society
- Minimizing the consequences of extravagance

UPBRINGING

A Muslim might have been raised in a family accustomed to extravagance and luxury. Growing up with this foundational habit of wastefulness makes it hard for someone to adjust to more humble ways of living, though Allah makes it easy for whomever He pleases. One Arab poet said, "A child can only grow as he's raised."

One of the antidotes to a habit of luxury is to direct the focus of those looking to get married on their potential spouse's piety, rather than their economic status. Notice Allah's emphasis on righteousness when He says,

وَأَنكِحُوا۟ ٱلْأَيَـٰمَىٰ مِنكُمْ وَٱلصَّـٰلِحِينَ مِنْ عِبَادِكُمْ وَإِمَآئِكُمْ

Marry off the singles among you, as well as the righteous of your bondmen and bondwomen. [24:32]

Allah also clearly prohibits us from marrying polytheists, a law which highlights the long-term importance of faith and similar priorities in a marriage:

وَلَا تَنكِحُوا۟ ٱلْمُشْرِكَـٰتِ حَتَّىٰ يُؤْمِنَّ وَلَأَمَةٌ مُّؤْمِنَةٌ خَيْرٌ مِّن مُّشْرِكَةٍ وَلَوْ أَعْجَبَتْكُمْ وَلَا تُنكِحُوا۟ ٱلْمُشْرِكِينَ حَتَّىٰ يُؤْمِنُوا۟ وَلَعَبْدٌ مُّؤْمِنٌ خَيْرٌ مِّن مُّشْرِكٍ وَلَوْ أَعْجَبَكُمْ أُو۟لَـٰٓئِكَ يَدْعُونَ إِلَى ٱلنَّارِ وَٱللَّهُ يَدْعُوٓا۟ إِلَى ٱلْجَنَّةِ وَٱلْمَغْفِرَةِ بِإِذْنِهِۦ وَيُبَيِّنُ ءَايَـٰتِهِۦ لِلنَّاسِ لَعَلَّهُمْ يَتَذَكَّرُونَ ۝

Do not marry polytheistic women until they believe; for a believing slave-woman is better than a free polytheist, even though she may look pleasant to you. And do not marry your women to polytheistic men until they believe, for a believing slave-man is better than a free polytheist, even though he may look pleasant to you. They call to the Fire while Allah calls to Paradise and forgiveness by His grace. He makes His revelations clear to the people so perhaps they will be mindful. [2:221]

Additionally, the Messenger of Allah ﷺ taught us that,

> A woman is married for four reasons: her wealth, her status, her beauty, or her piety. Choose the one with piety, and you shall prosper.[1]

WEALTH AFTER POVERTY

Attaining wealth after having suffered in poverty can lead someone to excessive consumption. Many people live deprived or extremely difficult childhoods, and then their circumstances change and they suddenly have access to wealth beyond anything they ever expected. People who experience this sudden shift usually have a hard time staying balanced in their consumption, suffering from a scarcity mindset after their conditions swung violently from one extreme to the other. Many of the most wealthy individuals in the world today have this "rags to riches" narrative, and often croon the story of their escape from poverty to luxury.

Our Wise Lord warns us against the glamour of this world for this very reason, teaching us to take from it moderately. His Messenger ﷺ said,

> Rejoice, and hope for that which delights you. By Allah, it is not poverty that I fear for you, but rather I fear for you that this world will be spread out to you like it was spread out for those before you, and you will compete for it just like they did—and it will destroy you just like it destroyed them.[2]

The Prophet ﷺ also said,

> This world is sweet and green. Allah has placed you as successors therein and will see how you act. So be mindful of this world, and be mindful with women, for the first tribulation of the Israelites was regarding women.[3]

EXTRAVAGANT FRIENDS

Spending time with people who are overly materialistic can also cause one to fall into extravagance. It is human nature to take on the qualities of those around us, especially of our long-time friends and companions. Those with stronger personalities tend to influence and affect the behavior of everyone around them. Thus, Islam is very emphatic on the importance of choosing one's company well.

NEGLECTING TO PREPARE FOR THE JOURNEY

Many fall into the trap of extravagance by failing to take the necessary precautions against it. The road to Allah's pleasure and Paradise is not paved with silk and lined with roses. Rather it is full of thorns and tears, stained with sacrifice and littered with potholes. Luxury will do us no benefit on a path whose toll is courage, endurance, and austerity. To undertake this journey we must be prepared for the weathering of its elements, and an extravagant lifestyle can be a severe hindrance.

This rigour is a defining quality of the stories of every prophet and righteous caller to Islam. Allah calls us to draw on their stories for inspiration—and to calibrate our expectations—when He says,

أَمْ حَسِبْتُمْ أَن تَدْخُلُوا۟ ٱلْجَنَّةَ وَلَمَّا يَأْتِكُم مَّثَلُ ٱلَّذِينَ خَلَوْا۟ مِن قَبْلِكُم مَّسَّتْهُمُ ٱلْبَأْسَآءُ وَٱلضَّرَّآءُ وَزُلْزِلُوا۟ حَتَّىٰ يَقُولَ ٱلرَّسُولُ وَٱلَّذِينَ ءَامَنُوا۟ مَعَهُۥ مَتَىٰ نَصْرُ ٱللَّهِ أَلَآ إِنَّ نَصْرَ ٱللَّهِ قَرِيبٌ ۝

Do you think you will be admitted into Paradise without being tested like those before you? They were afflicted with suffering and adversity and were so shaken that the Messenger and the believers with him cried out, "When will Allah's help come?" Indeed, Allah's help is near. [2:214]

Allah advises us in the Quran to be prepared for the challenges ahead and not to grow too comfortable with temporary enjoyments:

أَمْ حَسِبْتُمْ أَن تَدْخُلُوا۟ ٱلْجَنَّةَ وَلَمَّا يَعْلَمِ ٱللَّهُ ٱلَّذِينَ جَٰهَدُوا۟ مِنكُمْ وَيَعْلَمَ ٱلصَّٰبِرِينَ ۝

Did you think you would enter the Garden without God first proving which of you would struggle for His cause and remain steadfast? [3:142]

FAMILY PRESSURE

Allah may test Muslims working for Islam with a spouse, child, or other family member who has extravagant habits and tendencies, demanding more than what is balanced. If we find ourselves in this predicament and do not counterbalance their behaviors with moderation, they will negatively affect us over time. The excessive habits of the people we live with can eventually make us excessive just like them.

Islam's emphasis on choosing a righteous spouse may prevent us from falling into this trap. There is a pressing need for the Muslim to be cautious in how they raise their families. Allah says,

يَٰٓأَيُّهَا ٱلَّذِينَ ءَامَنُوا۟ قُوٓا۟ أَنفُسَكُمْ وَأَهْلِيكُمْ نَارًا وَقُودُهَا ٱلنَّاسُ وَٱلْحِجَارَةُ عَلَيْهَا مَلَٰٓئِكَةٌ غِلَاظٌ شِدَادٌ لَّا يَعْصُونَ ٱللَّهَ مَآ أَمَرَهُمْ وَيَفْعَلُونَ مَا يُؤْمَرُونَ ﴿٦﴾

Believers! Protect yourselves and your families from a Fire whose fuel is people and stones, overseen by formidable and severe angels, who never disobey whatever Allah orders—always doing as commanded. [66:6]

The Prophet ﷺ also made clear to us our duty in the upbringing of those for whom we are responsible. He said,

> Each of you is a shepherd, and each of you will be questioned about his flock. The leader of a people is a shepherd, and he will be questioned for his flock. The man is a shepherd over his household, and he will be questioned about his flock. The woman is a shepherd over the home of her husband and his children, and she will be asked about them...[4]

MISUNDERSTANDING THE NATURE OF LIFE

Not paying mind to the nature of life and the world around us can lead us to being excessive and extravagant. Nothing in this life is meant to be permanent, and this earth is not where we are supposed to settle—being oblivious to this causes some of us to invest too much into this temporary and transient world. What is good for you today might be bad for you tomorrow. This is why Allah says,

وَتِلْكَ ٱلْأَيَّامُ نُدَاوِلُهَا بَيْنَ ٱلنَّاسِ

We alternate these days among people... [3:140]

We were meant to operate in this life with caution. There's always a chance that we may lose everything we enjoy and take pleasure in. Thus it is important to put away any excess resources we have for a time when we may need them. This goes beyond wealth and applies to being conscientious in how we use our time and health. To let these blessings slip from our hands is a reckless way of living and will undoubtedly lead to regret.

WEAK WILLPOWER

An inability to control the *nafs* (one's ego and desire) is often a cause of extravagance, excessiveness, and overspending. The *nafs* is always pulling at its chains and asking to be indulged, and without constant vigilance, it will break loose. If Muslims working for Islam give into their *nafs* and respond to its every request, it can lead them down a destructive path of indulgence and excess.

$$ \{ \text{نفس} \} $$

Nafs: the self; the ego and source of desires. Sometimes
in the Quran, *nafs* may refer to the human soul. The *nafs*
may be inspired with good or evil tendencies.

With this in mind, we can understand why Islam focuses on the internal fight against our own *nafs*, and why it takes precedence over any other endeavor. Allah says,

$$ \text{إِنَّ ٱللَّهَ لَا يُغَيِّرُ مَا بِقَوْمٍ حَتَّىٰ يُغَيِّرُوا مَا بِأَنفُسِهِمْ} $$

*Indeed, Allah would never change a people's state until they change
their own state.* [13:11]

In the longest continuous oath in the Quran, Allah vows about the human soul that,

$$ \text{قَدْ أَفْلَحَ مَن زَكَّىٰهَا ۞ وَقَدْ خَابَ مَن دَسَّىٰهَا ۞} $$

*Successful indeed is the one who purifies it, and doomed is the one
who corrupts it!* [91:9-10]

He also says,

$$ \text{وَٱلَّذِينَ جَٰهَدُوا۟ فِينَا لَنَهْدِيَنَّهُمْ سُبُلَنَا ۚ وَإِنَّ ٱللَّهَ لَمَعَ ٱلْمُحْسِنِينَ} $$

*As for those who struggle in Our cause, We will surely guide them
along Our Way. And Allah is certainly with the good-doers.* [29:69]

IGNORING THE SEVERITY OF THE DAY OF RESURRECTION

The Day of Resurrection is full of frightful scenes, some which are described vividly in the Quran. Being unmindful of the shocking reality of that Day can lead one to indulge in the comforts and luxuries of this world beyond the appropriate boundaries. Constant contact with the Quran will help us realize how grave the matter is, and how urgently we must shift our focus from our comfort and security in this world to our comfort and security on that day.

If we remind ourselves often of the Day of Resurrection and contemplate over its staggering reality, it would be hard for us to justify to ourselves indulgence in excessive luxuries. This mindset prevents us from veering too far away from reality into heedless amusement. Remembering death and the Day of Judgment keeps us in check, allowing us to see the traps of extravagance and preventing us from slipping down into more evil sins.

Take as our model our beloved Prophet ﷺ. He was exemplary in his disinterest in luxury while also being deeply engaged and invested in the wellbeing of those around him. His spirit and energy emanated from his consciousness, fear, and closeness to God, not from an attachment to the material. He once said, *"If you knew what I knew, you would laugh little and cry much."*[5] He added in another wording of the narration, *"... and you would not even be able to enjoy your spouses in bed."*[6]

FORGETTING THE REALITIES OF HUMAN SOCIETY

Humans today are standing on the edge of an abyss. The ground beneath them is about to quake, plunging them down into eternal depths. Muslims especially are living in a pitiful state of repression, and living in it can cause someone who lacks true perception to compensate exclusively through material means. They consume and indulge in order to forget their sad reality and the state of their communities and world. They fail to realize that the scale for success is multidimensional, and material wealth is only a minor component.

Allah teaches us throughout the Quran that our success is not in our numbers, and that the worldly status of the believers is not an indicator of their status with Him. He says to the Prophet ﷺ,

فَلَعَلَّكَ بَـٰخِعٌ نَّفْسَكَ عَلَىٰٓ ءَاثَـٰرِهِمْ إِن لَّمْ يُؤْمِنُواْ بِهَـٰذَا ٱلْحَدِيثِ أَسَفًا ۝

Now, perhaps you will grieve yourself to death over their denial, if they disbelieve in this message. [18:6]

And He says,

لَعَلَّكَ بَـٰخِعٌ نَّفْسَكَ أَلَّا يَكُونُوا مُؤْمِنِينَ ۝

Perhaps you will grieve yourself to death over their disbelief. [26:3]

Allah also instructs His Prophet,

فَلَا تَذْهَبْ نَفْسُكَ عَلَيْهِمْ حَسَرَٰتٍ

So do not waste yourself in regret over them. [35:8]

MINIMIZING THE CONSEQUENCES OF EXTRAVAGANCE

Despite its glamorous shell, living extravagantly carries many consequences that are destructive; they will be mentioned in detail in the next section. This common tendency to fall into traps without fully realizing their true harm is the reason that Islam makes patently clear the objectives and wisdoms behind most of its rulings and legislation. The amenities of a materialistic, consumer-oriented culture encourages us to indulge in much more than our actual needs. We begin to take for granted the mentality: "I want, therefore I must have."

With details that are both entertaining and full of insight, the Companion Jabir ibn Abdallah retells this story. One day Jabir had some extra money and was sent out by his family to the market to buy a treat. Umar ibn Al-Khattab observed Jabir carrying money in his hand, and asked where he was headed. Jabir said that he was off to buy some meat for his family because they desired it. Upon this, Umar ranted incredulously, "Whenever you desire, you buy?! Do you fill your belly apart from your cousin and your neighbor? What about the verse of the Quran: *"You squandered the good things you were given in your earthly life, you took your fill of pleasure there..."*? [46:20] Jabir concluded his story with these words: "I wish the money had fallen from my hand, and I had not that day run into Umar!" While we may smile at Jabir's dismay and marvel at Umar's drastic reaction, this story highlights the disparities in consumption and the fulfilment of desire. According to the standards of Umar, we do indeed fill our bellies apart from our neighbors on a daily basis.

Effects of Extravagance

The harms of extravagance are plenty, and one does not have to look too far to see the extensive damage that it does not just to individuals, but to Islamic work and society. Some of the ways that extravagance can affect us individually and collectively include:

- Weakening the body
- Hardening the heart
- Feebleness of the mind
- Paving the way for sin
- Failure when tested with hardship
- Lack of empathy
- Severe questioning on Day of Judgment
- Falling into prohibited means of income
- Taking on satanic qualities
- Being denied Allah's Love

WEAKENING THE BODY

The most apparent negative effect that living in excess has on us is how weak it makes us physically. Our bodies are governed by the constants and standards that Allah created them upon, and if we deviate from them with either excess or deprivation, we will only stunt our own strength and growth. This then leads the Muslim to begin to fall short in obligations and responsibilities.

HARDENING THE HEART

Excessive indulgence in luxury also leads to a hard heart. Our hearts soften when we are hungry or undernourished because we feel more vulnerable, and so when we fill our stomachs and satisfy every craving we have, our hearts grow harder. This is Allah's way,

$$\text{فَلَن تَجِدَ لِسُنَّتِ ٱللَّهِ تَبْدِيلًا}$$

You will find no change in the way of Allah... [35:43]

A hard heart can hold us back from doing good deeds and obeying Allah, and so He tells us how doomed the hard-hearted are:

$$\text{فَوَيْلٌ لِّلْقَٰسِيَةِ قُلُوبُهُم مِّن ذِكْرِ ٱللَّهِ}$$

So woe to those whose hearts are hardened at the remembrance of Allah! [39:22]

Even when a Muslim strives against his own inclinations and performs acts of rightousness and obedience, he will not find any sweetness in them if his heart is hard. This is why the Messenger of Allah ﷺ warned us against being among those who pray at night, *"but all they get out of it is lack of sleep."*[7] A heart hardened by excessive comfort and luxury will have a hard time finding the same pleasure in physical worship and strenuous work for the good of Islam.

FEEBLENESS OF THE MIND

There are many components within us that contribute to our mental energy and fortitude. One vital component is the stomach. When the stomach is empty, the mind is more sharp and active, but when it is full, it is weighed down by lethargy. This is why Benjamin Franklin writes in *Poor Richard's Almanac*, "Hold your council before dinner; the full belly hates thinking as well as acting."

The fraility of the mind caused by the full stomach can prevent a Muslim from benefitting from their studies and deter them in actually putting their knowledge to action. Being that our advanced ability to learn and develop complex ideas is what separates us from the rest of creation, we must be keen not to lose it. And being that a sharp mind is required for excellence in any field, let alone in Islamic work, we cannot afford to compromise it for a few extra bites of food.

PAVING THE WAY FOR SIN

Living with a full stomach, counting the minutes until the next indulgent meal, drink, or snack, subjects us to falling more easily into sin.

41

Extravagance builds a certain tolerance within us for things that harm our souls. Excessive consumption in all of its forms activates the latent desire for what Allah prohibited. Muslims can easily find themselves slipping slowly down the path of sin with less ability to resist its gravity due to the indulgent lifestyle to which they have become accustomed. It would only be by Allah's mercy that they come out safe.

Notice what is prescribed in Islam for young people with fervent desires who can'tget married: fasting. The Messenger of Allah ﷺ said,

> Young people! Whoever among you has the ability should get married, for it is more conducive to lowering the gaze and protecting the private parts. Whoever cannot must then fast, for it will keep them chaste.[8]

FAILURE WHEN TESTED WITH HARDSHIP

There are times in which we may encounter more hardship and physical strain than we are accustomed to. Those who spend their lives in comfort and luxury have an especially hard time adjusting to their new conditions and are often unable to endure their trials successfully. Those who do survive, regardless of their lifestyle or background, only do so by Allah's help, and Allah only helps those who strive against their own souls and seek His pleasure diligently.

Thus it was for the group of Companions who set out during times of severe hardship with the Messenger of Allah ﷺ and pledged allegiance and loyalty to him despite the low chances of success. Allah granted them His pleasure, aid, and serenity:

$$لَّقَدْ رَضِىَ ٱللَّهُ عَنِ ٱلْمُؤْمِنِينَ إِذْ يُبَايِعُونَكَ تَحْتَ ٱلشَّجَرَةِ فَعَلِمَ مَا فِى قُلُوبِهِمْ فَأَنزَلَ ٱلسَّكِينَةَ عَلَيْهِمْ وَأَثَابَهُمْ فَتْحًا قَرِيبًا ۝$$

Indeed, Allah was pleased with the believers when they pledged allegiance to you under the tree. He knew what was in their hearts, so He sent down serenity upon them and rewarded them with a victory at hand [48:18]

LACK OF EMPATHY

As human beings, we are rarely ever concerned for the wellbeing of anyone other than ourselves. But in a state of hunger and exhaustion, we are able to empathize with those who live in deprivation. Living a lifestyle wherein we satisfy every craving that arises can make us numb to the suffering of others and oblivious to their needs.

It is recorded about the Prophet Yusuf that when he was in the position of ministry over the resources of Egypt, he never ate until he was full. When someone asked him why he withheld from himself such a simple indulgence, he said, "I am afraid that if I get full, I will forget about the hungry." How can someone who is engulfed in comfort and extravagance from every direction think or care about anyone else?

SEVERE QUESTIONING ON THE DAY OF JUDGMENT

There will come a day when we will have to stand in front of Allah and answer for all that we spent and consumed. Allah says,

$$ ثُمَّ لَتُسْـَٔلُنَّ يَوْمَئِذٍ عَنِ ٱلنَّعِيمِ ۝ $$

Then, on that Day, you will definitely be questioned about pleasures.
[102:8]

The following story illustrates how the thought of being questioned on the Day of Judgment for something as simple as a single meal frightened the Companions and spurred them to action.

The Prophet ﷺ came out to the mosque one day in the scorching midday heat, a time that most people would use for a short nap, and found Abu Bakr and Umar there. "What is it that brings you both out of your houses at this time?" he asked. "Hunger, Messenger of Allah," they replied in desperation.

The Prophet ﷺ admitted that it was the same pain that kept him from being able to rest, and so they went to visit Abu Ayyoob, a man from the Ansar who used to take great pleasure in sharing what he had with the Prophet ﷺ, and always had some food and milk set aside for him.

When they reached Abu Ayyoob's door, his wife came out and said, "Welcome, Prophet of Allah, and to those who are with him!" The Prophet ﷺ asked her, "Where is Abu Ayyoob?" Abu Ayyoob heard the voice of the Prophet as he was working in his date plantation, so he came running. Embarrassed for not having his usual preparations ready for the Prophet's visit, he said, "Welcome, Prophet of Allah, and to those who are with him! This is not the usual time that you come!" The Prophet ﷺ said, "That is true."

Abu Ayyoob cut fruit from the palm trees, containing all varieties of dry, moist, and green dates. The Prophet ﷺ said, "I didn't intend this. You should have just picked the dry ones for us." He said, "Prophet of Allah, I want you to eat from the dry, the moist, and the green. I will also slaughter for you." He ﷺ said, "If you do slaughter, then do not slaughter an animal carrying milk." Abu Ayyoob then took a young goat and slaughtered it. He said to his wife, "Bake some dough for us, for you are better at baking." He took the goat and grilled half of it.

When the food was ready, Abu Ayyoob placed it before the Prophet and the Companions. The Prophet ﷺ then took a piece of meat and wrapped it in a loaf of bread. He said, "O Abu Ayyoob, send this to Fatimah, for she has not had anything like this in a long time." Abu Ayyoob then delivered it to Fatimah.

After they ate and were satisfied, the Prophet ﷺ exclaimed, his eyes tearing, "Bread, meat, dry dates, green dates, and moist dates! I swear by the One in whose hand is my soul, these are certainly the pleasures about which you will be asked!" and then he ﷺ recited the verse in Surah al-Takathur, *"Then, on that Day, you will definitely be questioned about (your worldly) pleasures."* (102:8)

This statement worried his Companions greatly, for they now felt guilty for indulging in what now appeared to be an extravagant luxury. The Prophet ﷺ noticed their dismay, and so he instructed them to say "In the name of Allah" (bismillah) before they eat, and afterwards to say, "All praise is due to Allah, who was the One who satisfied us, blessed us, and was generous to us" (al-hamdu lillâh il-ladhi huwa ashba'anâ wa an'ama 'alaynâ wa afdhal). He told them "This would suffice as a response."[9]

Notice how troubled the Companions were by such a simple meal, especially upon realizing that they would be questioned about it. What was a luxurious meal to them would be viewed today as commonplace. This is because we have become desensitized and ungrateful. We have forgotten the severity of our impending questioning on the Day of Resurrection, which the Prophet ﷺ described as torment in and of itself.

FALLING INTO PROHIBITED MEANS OF INCOME

Someone who lives extravagantly may push the boundaries of their own means with their spending and is likely to end up in financial difficulty or even bankruptcy. In order to sustain their lifestyle, they may draw income from impermissible sources. The Prophet ﷺ sternly warned against nourishing ourselves from unwholesome means, threatening that, *"The fire has more of a right over every body that grows from filth."*[10]

TAKING ON SATANIC QUALITIES

Allah warns against excessive spending all throughout the Quran. One of the most stern verses to address the issue is found in Surah *al-Isrā'*:

إِنَّ ٱلْمُبَذِّرِينَ كَانُوٓاْ إِخْوَٰنَ ٱلشَّيَٰطِينِ وَكَانَ ٱلشَّيْطَٰنُ لِرَبِّهِۦ كَفُورًا ۝

Surely the wasteful are brothers to the devils. And the Devil is ever ungrateful to his Lord. [17:27]

Those who spend and consume wastefully are described here as *"brothers"* to the devils, emphasizing how they become a part of Satan's grand scheme. Though they may feel like they are securing material wealth and reveling in their gains, they are actually setting themselves up for tragic loss. Allah says,

أَلَآ إِنَّ حِزْبَ ٱلشَّيْطَٰنِ هُمُ ٱلْخَٰسِرُونَ ۝

Surely Satan's party is bound to lose. [58:19]

BEING DENIED ALLAH'S LOVE

There are many paths to gaining Allah's love, but the path to losing it are very few. Thus there is no bigger failure than to disqualify yourself from Allah's love and compassion. Allah instructs us in the Quran to beautify ourselves for worship and to consume worldly goods moderately, and then says at the end of the ayah,

$$\text{إِنَّهُ لَا يُحِبُّ الْمُسْرِفِينَ}$$

Surely He does not like the wasteful. [7:31]

What is left for those who are deprived of Allah's love? They will live in a constant state of misery and disarray. They will suffer and feel pain within, no matter what material comforts and luxuries they might be surrounded by. Only divine love can fill that spiritual void.

Remedies for Extravagance

There are numerous ways to treat the causes and effects of extravagance. The methods discussed here are:

- Reflecting on the impact of extravagance
- Self-restraint
- Setting the sunnah as the standard
- Looking to examples of early Muslims
- Avoiding extravagant company
- Nurturing good family habits
- Keen understanding of reality
- Remembering death often
- Reflecting on the road ahead

1. Reflecting on the impact of extravagance
Taking time to ponder over and contemplate the negative consequences of excessive consumption, constant indulgence, and extravagance can help us overcome it. This will help us organically come to terms with the reality of its harms and create a natural aversion within us against it.

2. Self-restraint
A soul that is accustomed to luxury and comfort must be weaned off of such habits. We must train our wills against impulsive compliance to desire, learning to endure hardship and difficulty for a higher

purpose. This includes waking ourselves from the comfort of sleep in the middle of the night to pray before fajr, abstaining from food and drink outside of Ramadan for voluntary fasts, and parting with our hard-earned money in charity. These routine drills against our lusts will help us in developing strength to carry even heavier burdens when the need arises.

Reducing Consumption

Self-restraint allows us to be holistic in our approach to consumption, not only preventing extravagance but also giving things due spiritual weight. Take, for example, a shirt you wish to purchase. While the objective purchase of this shirt may be halal, an individual trained in self-restraint will consider other aspects of the shirt and its purchase. Perhaps the price of that shirt is unnecessarily high, and you are aware that you have not been balanced in your charity-giving. Perhaps the shirt was made in a sweatshop, in unsafe and unjust conditions. Perhaps you are only purchasing the shirt on an impulse, not because you truly need it.

Assessing our choices and restraining our desire through this lens also paints a more complex and meaningful worldview. We can begin to recognize that 1) rulings of halal and haram exist as guidelines but there are psycho-spiritual, contextual, economical, and personal layers beneath the basic binary, and 2) Every action and intention has weight and this breathes life into the most trivial of acts, aiding us in living a life that is wholly an act of worship.

3. Setting the sunnah as our standard

We must always look for guidance in the life of the Prophet ﷺ. He was the model for moderation in all regards, and embodied a practical balance of austerity and leniency. His story teaches us the value of self-restraint and tenacity in this world and struggling against the gravitational pull of our passions. For example, he taught us to hold ourselves to our own standards, rather than following the indulgent tendencies of others.

In a detailed narration, a guest who was an unbeliever came to the Messenger of Allah ﷺ, and so the Messenger of Allah ﷺ had a goat milked for him. He drank its milk, and then drank another, and then drank another, until he drank the milk of seven goats. The next day, he became Muslim, and so the Messenger of Allah ﷺ asked for another goat. He drank its milk, but then when he called for another goat, he could not finish its milk. The Messenger of Allah ﷺ then said, *"The believer eats with one organ while the disbeliever eats with seven organs."*[11]

The Prophet ﷺ also gave clear instructions on how much is appropriate for us to eat. He said,

> A human being does not fill any container worse than the stomach. Just some bites to straighten his back should be enough for a person. If he must, then let a third be for food, a third for drink, and a third for air.[12]

To show that the Messenger of Allah actually lived by these principles, Aishah once told her nephew Urwah, "We used to see three new moons pass—two whole months—without a fire being kindled in the Messenger of Allah's home." Urwah asked her, "What did you used to live off of?" She said, "The two staple foods: dates and water. But the Messenger of Allah did have some neighbors from the Ansar who had goats, and so they would lend the goats' milk to the Messenger of Allah, and he would give it to us to drink."[13]

Aishah also recounts, "The mattress of the Messenger of Allah was made of animal hide and stuffed with palm fiber. The family of Muhammad never ate their fill of wheat foods for three consecutive days from when he arrived in Madina until he passed away."[14]

We must keep in mind that this was not due to the Prophet's ﷺ inability to provide for his family. This was the lifestyle he chose to be the model for Muslims until the end of time. He actually prayed for these circumstances, as he knew the dangers of excessive wealth and consumption. He would supplicate to Allah: *"Allah, give Muhammad's family sustenance that is sufficient."*[15]

Muslims working for Islam must take this into consideration when developing their personal habits and raising their families. These snapshots from the Prophet's life are meant not only to stir our emotions but also transform how we live. His path is the ultimate model for us to follow, and we do so hoping to attain his company in Paradise.

وَمَن يُطِعِ ٱللَّهَ وَٱلرَّسُولَ فَأُوْلَٰٓئِكَ مَعَ ٱلَّذِينَ أَنْعَمَ ٱللَّهُ عَلَيْهِم مِّنَ ٱلنَّبِيِّـۧنَ
وَٱلصِّدِّيقِينَ وَٱلشُّهَدَآءِ وَٱلصَّٰلِحِينَ ۚ وَحَسُنَ أُوْلَٰٓئِكَ رَفِيقًا ۝ ذَٰلِكَ ٱلْفَضْلُ
مِنَ ٱللَّهِ ۚ وَكَفَىٰ بِٱللَّهِ عَلِيمًا ۝

And whoever obeys Allah and the Messenger will be in the company
of those blessed by Allah: the prophets, the people of truth, the
martyrs, and the righteous—what honourable company! This is
Allah's favor, and Allah fully knows. [4:69-70]

4. *Looking to the examples of early Muslims*

Our tradition, starting from the Companions and spanning centuries of righteous scholars, is filled with heroes for us to take as role models. They lived humble lives, not assigning any more value to this world than it deserved. They knew it only to be a bridge to the afterlife.

In an instance that is reminiscent of the story recounted earlier by Jabir, Umar bin al-Khattab once visited his son Abdullah and saw that he was eating meat. "What is this meat?" Umar asked. Abdullah responded, "I was craving it." Perturbed, Umar said, "Do you really eat whatever you crave? To eat whatever you crave is enough to be called extravagant!"[16]

In a similar situation amidst the Companions, Salman al-Farisi came to see Abu Bakr during the illness from which he eventually died. Painfully imagining the world with the absence of a man of the stature of Abu Bakr, Salman requested some parting advice from him. Abu Bakr said, "Allah will open this world for you. Only take from it what you need to reach your ultimate destination."[17]

When he was governor over Kufa, Sa'd bin Abu Waqqās wrote a letter to Umar bin al-Khattab requesting permission to build a house for himself to live in. Umar granted him permission, but gave him some guidelines: "Build what will protect you from the sun and keep you dry from the rain. This world is only a vehicle."[18]

When those of us who are involved in Islamic work come across these stories, they should kindle a fire within us to follow this same path of moderation and detachment from material delights. We should realize through these powerful scenes of austerity that no matter our financial status, we cannot spiritually afford to get caught in this trap of extravagance. With this newfound ambition, we can rid ourselves of our excessive tendencies and work towards building the resilience and tenacity of those who bore the torch of this religion all throughout history.

5. Avoiding extravagant company

Choosing to spend our time with people of high ambitions, beyond the success of this life, will force us to develop new standards for our habits and lifestyles. Such people live a paradigm of striving and nobility, declining to conform to the base and excessive norms of the majority. This new way of living that we can learn from those role models will help us protect not only our wealth, but also our honor and even our lives. It is a lifestyle that embodies God's perfectly balanced laws.

Instead of spending time with spendthrifts who live for instant gratification, comparing livelihoods, and amassing more material goods, we must find people who live moderately within their means and invest in the life that is better and longer lasting. These are people who don't care what happens to them so long as God is pleased with them. Though finding such people may be hard, these are the people whom we need to help us in perfecting the Prophetic model of austerity.

6. Nurturing good family habits

Ridding our homes and families of the disease of excessive consumption helps prevent us from falling back into the habits that we manage to drop. Building our families upon moderation and balance makes the path smoother and free of the temptations of luxury that might catch us on our journey. And so we tread that path together to our Lord, with whom comfort and luxury is everlasting.

7. Keen understanding of reality

Looking around us and thinking deeply about our current condition, especially for Muslims as a whole, helps us defeat our excessive tendencies. Someone who is well aware and always mindful of the suffering of poverty and injustice cannot find it in their hearts to be wasteful with their time and resources. Our sympathy for the Muslims around the world should motivate us to use all that we possess to restore the honor and excellence that was once emblematic of Islam.

This sympathy was prescribed by the Prophet 🙵 when he said, *"The believers, in their mutual love, compassion, and affection, are like a single body. When one limb feels pain, the rest of the body suffers from restlessness and fever."*[19]

8. Remembering death often

Remembering the frightful sights of death and all that comes after it helps eradicate excessive habits from our daily lives. If we internalize the urgency and gravity of our inevitable deaths, we will find it hard to justify indulgence in luxuries. Our priorities will center around preparing for our departure instead of being preoccupied by self-gratification and hedonistic pleasures.

9. Reflecting on the road ahead

The journey we embarked on when we chose the path of Islamic work is one of exhaustion and trials. Our destination cannot be reached by wasteful indulgence, excessive consumption, and luxury; rather, it requires resilience, tenacity, and grit. Accepting this is an important part of ridding ourselves of our wastefulness. Our struggle against our own whims and desires, and the obstacles and dangers of this road, can only be overcome through living the values of moderation, self-restraint, and prudence.

✤ ✤ ✤ ✤

ENDNOTES

1. al-Bukhari, v. 7, p. 9; Muslim, #1466
2. al-Bukhari, v. 8, p. 112; Muslim, #2961
3. Muslim, #2742
4. al-Bukhari, v. 9, p. 77; Muslim, #1829
5. al-Bukhari, v. 8, p. 127; Muslim, #2313
6. al-Tirmidhi, #2312
7. al-Haythami, Majma' al-Zawā'id, v. 3, p. 205
8. al-Bukhari, v. 7, p. 3; Muslim, #1400
9. Ibn Hibbān, #5216 (summarized)
10. al-Tirmidhi, #614
11. al-Bukhari, v. 7, p. 93; Muslim, #2063
12. al-Tirmidhi, #2380
13. al-Bukhari, v. 8, p. 121, 122; Muslim, #2972
14. al-Bukahri, v.9 p. 122; Muslim, #2970
15. al-Bukhari, v. 8, p. 122 (in this wording); Muslim, #1055
16. al-Kandahlawi, Hayāt al-Sahābah, v. 2, pp. 284, 285
17. Ibid., p. 287
18. Ibid., p. 286
19. Muslim, #2586

Haste & Impatience

Impatience in awaiting the results of our work can have many negative effects on the activist and the community. The word for this in Arabic is *Isti'jāl*, and it means linguistically to expect or demand something with haste. A derivative of the same root is used in the Quran in the following ayah:

وَلَوْ يُعَجِّلُ ٱللَّهُ لِلنَّاسِ ٱلشَّرَّ ٱسْتِعْجَالَهُم بِٱلْخَيْرِ لَقُضِىَ إِلَيْهِمْ أَجَلُهُمْ

If Allah were to hasten evil for people as they wish to hasten good, they would have certainly been doomed. [10:11]

People sometimes pray for things that are actually harmful, either knowingly out of rage or unwittingly. Allah assures us that we would have been destroyed as a race a long time ago if He granted everything as immediately and urgently as we expected of Him, for in our haste and ignorance we do not always know what is best for us.

In the context of our discussion, *isti'jal* refers to an approach that aims to change the world and the Muslim condition overnight. It is an unpragmatic and immature approach, blind to how the world works and the challenges that await us on this journey. People want to see quick progress and expect everything to improve within a short amount of time. Others think there is a magic formula that would create instantaneous change and transformation if everyone were to abide by it. Someone who approaches Islamic activism with this mindset is ill-prepared for their journey.

"I can see myself falling into this pitfall. It's only natural to want to see the fruit of your work. We are primed to make constant calculations of what is efficient and what has the highest impact. Maybe that comes from our schooling, where we learn to do just enough work to get the intended outcome and nothing more. I've thought long and hard about what I would like to do in my career and Islamic work, and in my decision-making, I factor in the impact of my work.

We always have in mind that we will change the entire world in a significant way. But this hasty, over-ambitious mindset leads me to feel helpless. Allah tells us that he does not judge us by the results but by the effort that we put in. The expectation is that we continue to put in effort from the present moment till the moment we die, regardless of whether we see the results in our lifetimes. I've begun using this mindset with my personal relationships and my dawah work, trying to spread positivity without expecting any reciprocation and possibly without seeing the effect it had on people's lives."

Haste is part of human nature and was installed within our nature by our Creator. Allah says,

خُلِقَ ٱلْإِنسَـٰنُ مِنْ عَجَلٍ

Humankind is made of haste. [21:37]

وَيَدْعُ ٱلْإِنسَـٰنُ بِٱلشَّرِّ دُعَآءَهُۥ بِٱلْخَيْرِ وَكَانَ ٱلْإِنسَـٰنُ عَجُولًا ۝

And humans pray for evil as they pray for good. For humankind is ever hasty. [17:11]

Haste isn't always a vice—it can be beneficial and even praise-worthy when the situation calls for it. Even in cases where haste is desirable, it must be accompanied by a careful calculation of conse-quences and a consideration of context. This requires skills, ability, and experience. Allah alludes to this when He tells us about His conversation with Moses. He asked:

وَمَآ أَعْجَلَكَ عَن قَوْمِكَ يَـٰمُوسَىٰ ۝ قَالَ هُمْ أُوْلَآءِ عَلَىٰٓ أَثَرِى وَعَجِلْتُ إِلَيْكَ رَبِّ لِتَرْضَىٰ ۝

Why have you come with such haste ahead of your people, O

Moses?" He replied, "They are close on my tracks. And <u>I have</u>
<u>hastened</u> to You, my Lord, so You will be pleased. [20:83-84]

Given the condition of his people, the rarity of the opportunity, and
his sincere intention, Moses could not hold himself back from hastening toward the meeting with his Lord.

The blameworthy haste is that which comes from seeking immediate gratification and is devoid of any planning or preparation. It is
an impatience with the natural course of Allah's plan, and an attempt
to bypass the necessary stages and trials of guidance, victory, and
Islamic work. This is the haste that our beloved Prophet ﷺ warned
against.

A Companion named Khabbāb bin al-Arat came to the Prophet ﷺ
complaining of the torture and pain that he and the other Muslims
were enduring at the time. He asked the Prophet ﷺ to pray to Allah
for triumph and victory, but the Prophet ﷺ told him,

> Men among those who came before you used to be placed in
> ditches in the ground, and then a saw would be brought and
> placed on his head, slicing him in half. That still would not
> deter him from his faith. They would be scathed with iron
> combs down to their bones or their nerves, and that would
> not deter them from their faith. By Allah, this matter will
> come to fruition, to the point that someone will ride from
> Sanaa to Hadhramaut fearing nothing but Allah, or fearing
> the wolf for his sheep. But you are hasty.[1]

Effects of Haste & Impatience

Hastening results comes with harmful effects and consequences. It
can lead, for example, to the burnout and decreased commitment
that was discussed previously. Someone who is impatient for results
has a hard time accepting that small and consistent actions are better
than actions that are grandiose but unsustainable. The Prophet ﷺ
himself said, *"The most beloved actions to Allah are the consistent
ones, even if they are small."*[2]

Haste can also be the reason that someone suffers a dishonorable
death. Ater leaving this world, there will be no way to come back
for a second chance, and the only thing ahead of us will be Allah's
questioning of how we used the resources and abilities that He gave
us. That will be the day when:

يَوْمَ لَا تَمْلِكُ نَفْسٌ لِنَفْسٍ شَيْئًا وَٱلْأَمْرُ يَوْمَئِذٍ لِلَّهِ ۝

*"No soul will be of benefit to another whatsoever, for all authority
on that Day belongs to Allah."* [82:19]

In the early years of the Islamic Movement in Egypt, there was a
young man who was full of excitement and zeal. His name was Ahmad
Rifat, and he held some critical views of the Muslim activists of his
time, voicing them at one of their meetings in the 1930s.

Rifat felt that there were a number of things that Muslim activists
were doing wrong. They were generally cooperative and compliant
with government restrictions and demands, something he felt was
hypocritical to the core values of the movement, citing the ayah that
most overzealous critics of cooperation and collaboration improperly
interpret:

وَمَن لَّمْ يَحْكُم بِمَآ أَنزَلَ ٱللَّهُ فَأُوْلَٰئِكَ هُمُ ٱلْكَٰفِرُونَ ۝

*And those who do not judge by what Allah has revealed are the
disbelievers.* [5:44]

Rifat's logic was that since the Egyptian government did not rule
according to Islamic law, anyone who cooperates with them was
to be considered an unbeliever. He had numerous other criticisms
and expressed impatience with the movement's focus on gradual
reform of individuals and community. Despite many who advised
him to look at the bigger picture and understand the context and
contemplate the divine laws of how change happens, he refused to
listen, convinced that he had the solution. Frustrated with activists
who supported the Palestinian cause only through material support,
he eventually took off on his own to fight for Palestinian liberation.
There, he was mistaken for an enemy informant and killed.

This is one of many examples in the histories of Islamic move-
ments when an impatience and lack of foresight caused problems
within the community. The ending of this particular story illustrates
the bitter results of a heedless haste. This was a zealous approach
rooted in a shallow understanding of God's scripture, the history of
change, and the realities of life. This unfortunate individual joined
the movement without having studied the Quran in-depth or the

life and teachings of the Prophet ﷺ, and developed his own individualistic perspective without grounding himself in foundational principles. The result was a premature approach that led to his own destruction. Haste and impatience are mindsets that can ruin an Islamic activist if not curbed by wise restraint.

Haste and impatience can also be the reason why projects are not completed or delayed for decades. Many gains in Islamic work are reached through small, incremental steps, a reality which the hasty worker has little tolerance for. The result is that many of our community's efforts and projects are short-sighted and run in haphazard spurts, quickly abandoned when the payoff doesn't happen soon enough. It is one of the reasons so many projects and initiatives are "long overdue." Although we recognize their necessity; the effort required for these initiatives is too daunting and long-term for most impatient volunteers.

Causes of Haste & Impatience

Knowing the dangers that haste can lead to, we must look into what causes such a phenomenon among Islamic workers so that we can work toward eradicating it within ourselves and the culture of our organizations and communities. Some of the causes of haste and impatience are:

- Selfish impulses
- Religious fervor
- Cultural trends
- Fear of our opponents
- Being oblivious to opponents' tactics
- Widespread vice
- Inability to endure difficulties of the path
- Prioritizing the means over the end
- Lack of structure
- Lack of mentorship
- Being oblivious to Allah's patterns
- Forgetting our objective
- Forgetting the swiftness of Allah's justice

SELFISH IMPULSES

The tendency to haste is one that is built into our internal programming as humans.

$$خُلِقَ ٱلْإِنسَـٰنُ مِنْ عَجَلٍ$$

Humankind is made of haste. [21:37]

In our haste and impatience, we get frustrated and sometimes call upon Allah to bring about what is truly bad for us.

$$وَيَدْعُ ٱلْإِنسَـٰنُ بِٱلشَّرِّ دُعَآءَهُ بِٱلْخَيْرِ وَكَانَ ٱلْإِنسَـٰنُ عَجُولًا ۝$$

And humans pray for evil as they pray for good. For humankind is ever hasty. [17:11]

Allah in His protection and care for us has caused good and evil to come in their own times and at a preordained pace, untied to our impatience and whims.

$$وَلَوْ يُعَجِّلُ ٱللَّهُ لِلنَّاسِ ٱلشَّرَّ ٱسْتِعْجَالَهُم بِٱلْخَيْرِ لَقُضِيَ إِلَيْهِمْ أَجَلُهُمْ$$

If Allah were to hasten evil for people as they wish to hasten good, they would have certainly been doomed. [10:11]

Often, our impatience can be due to an egocentric desire to bask in the fulfillment and satisfaction of our work firsthand, although our reward is not tied to results. Our desires and hopes drive us, instead of being bridled by the reins of our intellect.

RELIGIOUS FERVOR

When faith grows and overtakes the soul, it engenders an unparalleled driving force that can propel us towards so many sources of good. Sometimes, however, this motivation can lead to immature zeal, which causes harm when devoid of understanding and nuance. This is the wisdom behind Allah's choice to test and instruct the Prophet ﷺ and the believing community with patience and forbearance in the early years of Islam. Allah says in one of the earliest surahs to be revealed,

وَٱصۡبِرۡ عَلَىٰ مَا يَقُولُونَ وَٱهۡجُرۡهُمۡ هَجۡرࣰا جَمِيلًا ۞

Be patient with what they say, and depart from them courteously.
[73:10]

Allah also says,

فَٱصۡبِرۡ إِنَّ وَعۡدَ ٱللَّهِ حَقࣱّ وَلَا يَسۡتَخِفَّنَّكَ ٱلَّذِينَ لَا يُوقِنُونَ ۞

*So be patient, for the promise of Allah certainly is true. And do not
be disturbed by those who have no sure faith.* [30:60]

وَجَعَلۡنَا بَعۡضَكُمۡ لِبَعۡضࣲ فِتۡنَةً أَتَصۡبِرُونَ وَكَانَ رَبُّكَ بَصِيرࣰا ۞

*We have made some of you a trial for others. Will you be patient?
And your Lord is All-Seeing.* [25:21]

CULTURAL TRENDS

Haste could also be a product of one's time and place. Time itself
seems to pass astonishingly quickly in this era that we live in. Everything moves fast, and there is a prevalent obsession with efficiency
and expedience. We can be on one side of the Atlantic Ocean and
find ourselves on the other in a matter of hours. We can purchase
what we desire and often have it delivered within the span of a day
or less. Speed and convenience are golden standards in the eyes of
so many people.

But there are many things in life that we cannot speed up, and
when we try to, they backfire. Our generation's expectations of
instant gratification and immediacy often facilitate a culture of impatience. There is little tolerance for incremental work, and excellence
is often traded for expedient, flashy results. The results of that deficit
in effort are superficial gains and insubstantial progress.

FEAR OF OUR OPPONENTS

The sustained assault by those who work for evil and oppression can
understandably foster impatience and haste in the hearts of Islamic
workers. Islamophobia mounts rapidly, and uncountable lives are
lost daily due to unjust warmongering and hate. There is hardly any

place on earth where one can speak about the transformative and impactful values of Islam without someone trying to silence them. There should be no doubt in our minds that there are forces working night and day around the globe for the destruction of Islam, Muslims, and all prospects for peace and justice on earth.

Witnessing this reality sparks an impatience in the hearts of young activists, striking a chord that demands immediate change. With such dark clouds convening on the horizon, a hasty mind may think grand gestures more appropriate than gradual, patient work. But the most meaningful, impactful change never happens instantaneously. We may have to lay the foundations for projects and work which may or may not reach their final phase in our lifetimes.

BEING OBLIVIOUS TO OPPONENTS' TACTICS

Those who are working against Islam are employing a variety of filthy tactics to corrupt the heart of the global Muslim community and stunt its growth. Of the most effective of their tactics is to support (or perhaps even create) groups that call themselves Muslim while having no real foundation in the religion.

These groups range from the watered-down to the overzealous and extreme; they capitalize on the impatience and frustration of those who are immature, impatient, and uneducated. They appeal to young and vulnerable minds, luring them into either harming themselves or causing strife in the community. After a certain point, no further external intervention is necessary, and the poison spreads organically in the minds of the youth in various communities.

WIDESPREAD VICE WITH NO METHODOLOGY FOR CHANGE

Being surrounded by evil without understanding how to preempt and guard against its negative effects can easily lead a person into the trap of haste. In our times, there is no way to avoid exposure to vice. It is the Muslim's duty to act in order to remove the evil of their surroundings and provide alternatives. Allah says,

وَلَوْلَا دَفْعُ ٱللَّهِ ٱلنَّاسَ بَعْضَهُم بِبَعْضٍ لَّفَسَدَتِ ٱلْأَرْضُ وَلَٰكِنَّ ٱللَّهَ ذُو

فَضْلٍ عَلَى ٱلْعَلَمِينَ ۞

Had Allah not repelled a group of people by another, corruption
would have dominated the earth, but Allah is Gracious to all. [2:251]

He also said,

وَلَوْلَا دَفْعُ ٱللَّهِ ٱلنَّاسَ بَعْضَهُم بِبَعْضٍ لَّهُدِّمَتْ صَوَامِعُ وَبِيَعٌ وَصَلَوَاتٌ
وَمَسَاجِدُ يُذْكَرُ فِيهَا ٱسْمُ ٱللَّهِ كَثِيرًا وَلَيَنصُرَنَّ ٱللَّهُ مَن يَنصُرُهُۥ إِنَّ ٱللَّهَ
لَقَوِيٌّ عَزِيزٌ ۞

Had Allah not repelled some people by means of others, destruction
would have surely claimed monasteries, churches, synagogues,
and mosques in which Allah's Name is often mentioned. Allah
will certainly help those who stand up for Him. Allah is truly All-
Powerful, Almighty. [22:40]

The Prophet ﷺ instructed us that when we see any act of evil, we
must change it with our hands. If we cannot do that, then we must
change it with our tongues, and if even that is not possible, then to
at least hate it with our hearts, which he said is *"the weakest form*
of iman."[3] He also offered us a metaphor to demonstrate the importance of speaking out against evil:

> The one who upholds Allah's boundaries and the one who
> crosses them are like a group of people who drew lots on a
> ship. Some received the upper deck while the others received
> the lower deck. Whenever the ones in the lower deck would
> take water to drink, they would pass by the ones on the
> upper deck, so they said, "We should just poke a hole for
> ourselves so as not to bother those above us." If they allow
> them to do this, then they will all perish, but if they held
> their hands back, they would all be safe together.[4]

It is true that not every misdeed must be addressed immediately,
especially if it will lead to greater harm. If this is the case, it is actually obligatory to refrain from speaking out or trying to change it.
That is why the very least is to hate the action with your heart while
not engaging in it. At this point, however, we still should be looking
for the most effective ways to stop it and take the first opportunity
to do so.

Consider the various scenes throughout the Prophet's ﷺ life wherein he embodied this wise method. He was appointed as a Prophet in Mecca while the Kaaba was filled with pagan idols, but he did not take it upon himself to remove them until the pagans surrendered over two decades later. He knew that if he were to attempt to destroy them from the first day, it would have fueled an aggressive reaction from the pagans, sending them further away from accepting his message and driving them deeper into their ignorance. The goal of the Prophet ﷺ and the theme of the revelation during those formative years was to nurture an internal strength and purity. Only after that was attained were they ready to physically purify Mecca of its paganistic ignorance and impurity. The Prophet ﷺ destroyed the idols with his own hand, repeatingly reciting,

$$وَقُلْ جَآءَ ٱلْحَقُّ وَزَهَقَ ٱلْبَٰطِلُ ۚ إِنَّ ٱلْبَٰطِلَ كَانَ زَهُوقًا ۝$$

And declare, "The truth has come and falsehood has vanished.
Indeed, falsehood is bound to vanish." [17:81]

The Prophet ﷺ once said to Aisha, *"Did you know that when your people built the Kaaba, they made it smaller than the foundations Abraham laid?"* She said, "Messenger of Allah, will you not return it to the foundation Abraham laid?" He said, *"Were it not for your people having just recently been unbelievers, I would have done it."*[5] Here the Prophet ﷺ refrained from rebuilding the Kaaba and returning it to the shape built by Abraham out of fear that it would lead to the greater harm of disunity and discord. In a similar narration he even says, *"If only your people were not so recently in ignorance, for I fear that their hearts would reject it."*[6]

We will not be held accountable for the sinful actions around us if we opt for silence out of fear that an abrupt, aggressive change would lead to something even more harmful. Meanwhile we seek an effective course of action, while rejecting the evil through the actions of the heart.

$$لَا يُكَلِّفُ ٱللَّهُ نَفْسًا إِلَّا وُسْعَهَا$$

Allah does not require of any soul more than what it can afford.
[2:286]

Allah also says,

$$فَٱتَّقُوا۟ ٱللَّهَ مَا ٱسْتَطَعْتُمْ وَٱسْمَعُوا۟ وَأَطِيعُوا۟ وَأَنفِقُوا۟ خَيْرًا لِّأَنفُسِكُمْ$$

So be mindful of Allah to the best of your ability, hear and obey, and spend in charity—that will be best for you. [64:16]

When Islamic workers and callers to Allah do not understand the methodology of change on a broad societal scale, they will adopt a hasty, simplistic approach to taking action against evil. They will assume they are sinful if they do not enact immediate change, when in truth the nature of change on that scale entails gradual, consistent work.

Counteract Evil Environments with Good Company

The same tools and media that have made vice so widespread have also made it easier to find righteous groups and people who swim against the current. Spending time with those who make us better Muslims lets us recharge and gives us a clearer look at our own wrongdoings, instead of being overwhelmed by the grim state of the world. Often, these righteous circles are characterized by a bright optimism and proactiveness, despite the ubiquity of oppression and sin. While it's important to take the time to speak out against what is wrong, spending too much time surrounded by vice can be detrimental and push us away from the right path instead of bringing others closer to it. Taking the time and effort to develop a circle of trusted friends and mentors can keep us on track and prevent us from becoming impatient and feeling suffocated by evil.

THE INABILITY TO ENDURE THE DIFFICULTIES OF THE PATH

Some beginners launch into the scene of Islamic work with such enthusiasm, hoping their fiery ambition will create immediate change in the world. Their courage, excitement, and proactiveness is admirable; and they feel ready to commit to this cause until their death. But they may not yet have what it takes to endure the exhaustion and toll of the journey. The path of dedicating oneself to God and working consistently for Islam over the course of a lifetime is a courageous path, but it is difficult and ridden with hardship. True commitment must be accompanied by patience, perseverance, and grit. A true devotee to any cause must practice these consistently.

The immature enthusiast may try to circumvent the difficulties of the path of Islamic work through haste and quick results. However, there is no shortcut, and upon discovering this fact, many individuals abandon their commitment, justifying their failure through a variety of excuses. Our contemporary context is full of examples of volunteers and workers dropping out prematurely. In many cases, this failure was due to impatience and haste—an unrealistic expectation that the task would be easy and ostensibly rewarding.

Those who succeed in their commitment will be tested, tried, and even harmed for the sake of Allah, but they always keep their end goal in mind. They expect to be rewarded in the hereafter for their patience and difficult experiences; this is their motivation to keep going. The conditions may not be ideal, the opportunities may not be abundant, and the consequences may not be pleasant, but Allah ultimately will grant them success and aid them.

In the history of our community, there are many examples of individuals who were blessed with patience and steadfastness, their feet planted firmly in the present but their eyes fixed on the horizon. They were harmed multiple times, physically, socially, emotionally, and otherwise, for the sake of the work. They remained committed over the decades, building, sacrificing, and charting a course for Islamic work that would extend beyond their lifetimes. Today's generation of Islamic workers and activists stand upon their shoulders and benefit from the security of the foundation laid for them.

PRIORITIZING THE MEANS OVER THE END

In Islamic activism, we often get too caught up with the process that we forget about the end goal. We tend to emphasize indicators like the number of participants, likes and views, or specific metrics and tools, while failing to keep the overarching goals in mind. This imbalanced focus can lead to a hasty approach to create results that may not mean much in the long run, or may actually be harmful and weaken the community from within.

This concept of remaining focused on the end goal can be found in the Islamic teaching to remain patient against the leaders who err (as long as they do not openly leave Islam). The Prophet ﷺ said,

> Whoever sees something from his leader that he dislikes must remain patient, for whoever splits from the community by a handspan only dies a death of Jāhiliyyah (ignorance).[7]

Frustration and impatience with leadership in the Muslim community is often due to secondary shortcomings—lack of management skills, limited vision, or difficult personalities. A hasty, impatient individual may become overly focused on these short-term obstacles, losing sight of long-term priorities such as the continuity of Islamic work and community stability.

The Companion 'Ubādah bin al-Sāmit recounts that the Prophet ﷺ once called upon them to pledge allegiance. Among what the Prophet ﷺ called for them to swear was,

> We pledge to hear and obey in times of high spirits and low spirits, in times of difficulty and ease, and even when we are not treated favorably. Also that we would not vye for power with those who have it unless we see blatant unbelief among us that is supported by evidence.[8]

Imam al-Nawawi says in his commentary on the hadith of 'Ubādah that the hadith means to not fight for power with those who hold it, and do not oppose them unless you see a verified act of evil that you know to be against the foundations of Islam. He writes, "If you see this, then advise them against it and speak the truth wherever you may be. But going out against them in arms and fighting them is prohibited by unanimous agreement of the Muslims, even if they are corrupt and unjust."[9] The Maliki scholar al-Dawudi said that it is mandatory to remove an unjust ruler who can be removed without creating chaos or leading to further injustice. Otherwise, it is mandatory to stay patient.[10]

LACK OF STRUCTURE

The lack of a structured model to channel the capabilities of Islamic workers early in their career can encourage an atmosphere of impatience. Volunteers and Islamic workers must be developed and moved from one phase of development to another, given positive experiences and outlets for their energy, and a chance to develop skills and learn.

Otherwise, the human soul is feeble and frail; if it is not occupied with the pursuit of good, it will occupy itself with falsehood.

Even in the spiritual aspect, small, consistent steps can be of more value than short-lived exuberance. This is why Islam provides us with a daily and nightly routine and worship rituals that are constantly recurring every week, month, and year. If we commit ourselves to these steady, incremental habits, our steps forward will be highly productive and fruitful.

It is the responsibility of Islamic leadership to ensure that every willing Muslim is able to contribute to beneficial, fruitful work, filling their hours with goodness and reward. The Prophet ﷺ said,

> Any leader who assumes leadership over the Muslims and then does not exert himself for them nor offer good counsel will not enter Paradise with them.[11]

LACK OF MENTORSHIP

When Islamic activists do their work without the guidance of those who have expertise and experience, it can quickly lead them into the trap of haste. Consider a newborn baby who knows nothing about the world they just entered. Allah says,

$$وَٱللَّهُ أَخْرَجَكُم مِّنۢ بُطُونِ أُمَّهَٰتِكُمْ لَا تَعْلَمُونَ شَيْـًٔا$$

And Allah brought you out of the wombs of your mothers while you knew nothing [16:78]

Then, through one of the means that Allah generously blessed them with, this child begins to learn. This learning is not from any book, but through experience and repetition. Just as a child observes its parents, we must benefit in our work from those who have tread the path before us, learning from their successes and mistakes in order to spare ourselves the pain of having to learn it at our own expense. Someone who is too proud or shy to ask and benefit from the experience of others will make a lot of unnecessary mistakes.

The concept of respecting and paying deference to the knowledgeable and experienced is a core value of our religion. It is the driving force in keeping our scripture and values as pristine as they were when Allah sent them down to the Prophet ﷺ. Knowledge even takes precedence over age and social status; both are still given their due consideration in Islam, but there are contexts which call for the precendence of knowledge over all else. The Prophet ﷺ said,

> Let the most well read in Allah's book among you lead you. If they are all equal in reading, then let it be the most knowledgeable of the Sunnah. If they are equal in the Sunnah, then let it be the one who migrated most long ago. If they are equal in their migration, then let it be the one who accepted Islam most long ago. A man should not lead another man in his own jurisdiction, nor should he sit in a special seat in the other's house, without his permission.[12]

The leadership hierarchy outlined in the hadith serves to highlight the value of knowledge and experience, and the importance of exercising deference to the experience and expertise of others.

BEING OBLIVIOUS TO ALLAH'S DIVINE WAYS AND PATTERNS

Not being mindful of the laws and patterns with which Allah creates the world around us and the souls within us can cause undue haste. It is easy to forget, for example, that Allah created the heavens and the earth in six days, and creates humans, animals, and plants in stages. All the while, He is fully capable of creating everything and more in a single moment.

$$إِنَّمَآ أَمْرُهُ إِذَآ أَرَادَ شَيْئًا أَن يَقُولَ لَهُۥ كُن فَيَكُونُ ۞$$

All it takes, when He wills something, is simply to say to it: "Be!"
And it is! [36:82]

We also learn from the way Allah created our souls that we can only sacrifice after we have refined ourselves internally. Allah says about the soul,

$$قَدْ أَفْلَحَ مَن زَكَّىٰهَا ۞ وَقَدْ خَابَ مَن دَسَّىٰهَا ۞$$

Successful indeed is the one who purifies it, and doomed is the one
who corrupts it! [91:9-10]

This is not an easy task, and its results don't manifest immediately.

Purifying the soul requires time, self-monitoring, practical application, and hard work.

The vital importance of taking our time with self-development and community development is also patently clear in how Allah legislated the laws of Islam during the life of the Prophet ﷺ. Drinking wine and engaging in usury were both gradually prohibited for the community, so as to first develop the hearts from within, preparing them for the external compliance with God's law. We must not forget this divine approach of steady and sustainable growth in our work.

FORGETTING OUR OBJECTIVE

Forgetting the ultimate goal towards which we are striving is perhaps one of the greatest causes of hastiness and impatience in the hearts of Islamic workers. Our goal is to seek the pleasure of Allah, and this only comes through abiding by His guidelines and not falling short in our responsibilities. It requires us to stay firm in our stance with unwavering devotion and sincerity until the Day of Resurrection. Even when the road stretches ahead and appears dismal, we remain constant to the teachings of our faith and do not seek out inappropriate shortcuts. As we march down the long path of service and commitment, this should be our motto:

$$\text{فَمَن كَانَ يَرْجُواْ لِقَآءَ رَبِّهِۦ فَلْيَعْمَلْ عَمَلًا صَٰلِحًا وَلَا يُشْرِكْ بِعِبَادَةِ رَبِّهِۦۤ أَحَدَۢا}$$

So whoever hopes for the meeting with their Lord, let them do good deeds and associate none in the worship of their Lord. [18:110]

This is true devotion and a promise that we will exert ourselves in putting our best foot forth for our Lord, complying with His orders as best as we can:

$$\text{فَٱتَّقُوا۟ ٱللَّهَ مَا ٱسْتَطَعْتُمْ}$$

So be mindful of Allah to the best of your ability... [64:16]

We will stand in front of our Lord and be questioned about whether or not we tried our best. Our salvation depends on it. We must not be worried about material results, as they are in the hands of Allah.

FORGETTING ABOUT ALLAH'S SWIFT JUSTICE

Another cause of haste and impatience is when we forget how Allah deals with wrongdoers and deniers. Not only does He threaten them with vengeance in His scripture, but a simple glance through history shows that Allah's justice is thorough and swift, despite seeming delayed from our perspective.

وَأُمْلِى لَهُمْ إِنَّ كَيْدِى مَتِينٌ ۞

I delay their end for a while, but My planning is flawless. [7:183]

وَرَبُّكَ ٱلْغَفُورُ ذُو ٱلرَّحْمَةِ لَوْ يُؤَاخِذُهُم بِمَا كَسَبُوا۟ لَعَجَّلَ لَهُمُ ٱلْعَذَابَ بَل لَّهُم مَّوْعِدٌ لَّن يَجِدُوا۟ مِن دُونِهِۦ مَوْئِلًا ۞

Your Lord is the All-Forgiving, Full of Mercy. If He were to seize them for what they commit, He would have certainly hastened their punishment. But they have an appointed time, from which they will find no refuge. [18:58]

When Allah seizes the tyrant, there is no escape. He says,

وَكَذَٰلِكَ أَخْذُ رَبِّكَ إِذَآ أَخَذَ ٱلْقُرَىٰ وَهِىَ ظَٰلِمَةٌ إِنَّ أَخْذَهُۥٓ أَلِيمٌ شَدِيدٌ ۞

Such is the grip of your Lord when He seizes the societies entrenched in wrongdoing. Indeed, His grip is painful and severe. [11:102]

وَلَا يَحْسَبَنَّ ٱلَّذِينَ كَفَرُوا۟ سَبَقُوٓا۟ إِنَّهُمْ لَا يُعْجِزُونَ ۞

Do not let those disbelievers think they are not within reach. They will have no escape. [8:59]

To offer us some relief in the seemingly long wait, Allah points out that time is one of His creations, and that what might seem to be a long reign of tyranny is negligible in the true scheme of things:

وَيَسْتَعْجِلُونَكَ بِٱلْعَذَابِ وَلَن يُخْلِفَ ٱللَّهُ وَعْدَهُۥ وَإِنَّ يَوْمًا عِندَ رَبِّكَ كَأَلْفِ سَنَةٍ مِّمَّا تَعُدُّونَ ۞

They challenge you to hasten the torment. And Allah will never fail in His promise. But a day with your Lord is indeed like a thousand years by your counting. [22:47]

When we forget this reality in our work, we will panic, assuming that our efforts are fruitless and pointless. We will justify our haste and impatience by saying that we must take drastic measures before the problem gets worse, or before the tyrant gains too much control. But Allah is in control, and He decides what is possible and what isn't.

INFLUENCE FROM IMPATIENT PEERS

Spending time with people who tend to rush and don't see value in taking time to do things with deliberation can affect how we approach matters as well. Habits spread among peers, and the attitudes of your friends will reflect on your own religious commitment. If we are not cautious about whom we take as our friends, we can end up falling into the trap of haste. This is perhaps why Islam emphasizes the need to be meticulous about whom we adopt as our companions, as addressed in previous sections.

Remedies for Haste and Impatience

After discussing the causes of impatience and haste, the remedies may be easy to surmise. They include:

- Comprehending the negative impact of haste
- Daily reflection on the Quran
- Close study of the Seerah
- Examining history
- Meaningful mentorship
- Acting according to a methodology and plan
- Understanding tactics of Islam's opponents
- Overcoming fear
- Disciplining the soul
- Keeping the goal in mind
- Self-awareness

1. Comprehending the negative impact of haste
Reading through the causes of haste and observing its negative effects around us can be enough to ward off its damage. You will naturally be deterred from it, firm and purposeful in your actions and

decisions. While reminding ourselves of the price of expediency, we may find that practicing patience and steadiness in our work and planning has a calming and grounding effect. Quality over quantity, and real, meaningful change and development is superior to hyperbole. Gradual, long-term gains make more of a difference than short-term fireworks. Do not make your work dependent on witnessing a shift in the tide. Rather, increase your endurance, capacity, and dedication to Allah so as to increase your contribution to His cause.

2. Daily reflection on the Quran

Maintaining a daily habit of contemplating Allah's scripture engrains the patterns with which He created the universe in our hearts. The more time we give to His book, the more we internalize the lessons He teaches therein. The more we learn about how Allah deals with injustice and wrongdoing, the less angst and impatience we will feel during the routine of daily life. This newfound peace affords us the strength and willpower necessary to stay the course. Allah says,

$$خُلِقَ ٱلْإِنسَـٰنُ مِنْ عَجَلٍ ۚ سَأُو۟رِيكُمْ ءَايَـٰتِى فَلَا تَسْتَعْجِلُونِ ۞$$

Humankind is made of haste. I will soon show you My signs, so do not ask Me to hasten them. [21:37]

$$ذَٰلِكَ ٱلْكِتَـٰبُ لَا رَيْبَ ۛ فِيهِ ۛ هُدًى لِّلْمُتَّقِينَ ۞$$

This is the Book! There is no doubt about it—a guide for those who are mindful [2:2]

$$إِنَّ هَـٰذَا ٱلْقُرْءَانَ يَهْدِى لِلَّتِى هِىَ أَقْوَمُ$$

Surely this Quran guides to what is most upright... [17:9]

3. Close study of the Seerah

Regular exposure to the pains and difficulties that the Prophet ﷺ faced, and seeing how he dealt patiently without ever acting out of haste, can prevent us from falling into this dangerous trap in our work. This is especially true when we consider that the Prophet ﷺ was ultimately given victory. Taking all of this into consideration in our work inspires us to follow suit and refrain from rushing results. Allah says,

لَّقَدۡ كَانَ لَكُمۡ فِى رَسُولِ ٱللَّهِ أُسۡوَةٌ حَسَنَةٌ لِّمَن كَانَ يَرۡجُواْ ٱللَّهَ وَٱلۡيَوۡمَ ٱلۡءَاخِرَ وَذَكَرَ ٱللَّهَ كَثِيرًا ۝

Indeed, in the Messenger of Allah you have an excellent example for whoever has hope in Allah and the Last Day, and remembers Allah often. [33:21]

4. Examining history

Familiarizing ourselves with history and the approach of those who have done this work before will help us see how they took their time with matters. Those who were successful throughout history usually had to endure a long waiting period before finally achieving their goals, and reminding ourselves of this fact helps us follow their example of endurance and deliberateness. There is a line of poetry that encourages the emulation of role models in history, even if we have not fully internalized their admirable qualities:

> *Emulate even if you do not compare to them,*
> *For the imitation of heroes is itself an achievement.*

After reading the stories of those who showed exemplary patience, we learn to speak and conduct ourselves as they would, until we eventually take ownership of their noble qualities of patience and consistency.

5. Meaningful Mentorship

Our work must be performed in the shade of those who have expertise and experience—those who have tread the path before us. This helps us calculate our every step and saves us energy and time. Learning from the mistakes of others helps us avoid unnecessary pains and burdens. The Prophet ﷺ alluded to this when he said, *"The believer is not stung from the same burrow twice."*[13]

6. Acting according to a methodology and plan

The importance of planning and methodology cannot be emphasized enough in the treatment of haste and impatience. We require meticulous plans and milestones for our spirituality, careers, Islamic work, and individual projects. We should ascribe to a methodology that takes us from one step to the next, fulfilling the needs of the moment while directing our energies to what is most productive and fruitful. We should not take a step forward except that both its direction and its distance are carefully designed to reach a specific goal.

7. Understanding the tactics of Islam's opposition
Predicting the tactics of evildoers helps us plan how we will react when we encounter them. It also forces us to reflect upon the long-term consequences of our decisions and strategies. Knowing the opponent's next steps gives us a chance to pace and prepare ourselves, while acting with wisdom and clarity.

8. Overcoming fear
We must not let the material power of Islam's opposition cripple us into inaction. This dynamic can reverse in a matter of moments, and that is not difficult for Allah to do. Allah instructs us clearly not to let apparent strength and prosperity deceive us from the reality of Who really is in control. In case we forget this reality, the Quran is full of reminders:

لَا يَغُرَّنَّكَ تَقَلُّبُ ٱلَّذِينَ كَفَرُواْ فِى ٱلْبِلَـٰدِ ۝ مَتَـٰعٌ قَلِيلٌ ثُمَّ مَأْوَىٰهُمْ جَهَنَّمُ وَبِئْسَ ٱلْمِهَادُ ۝

Do not be deceived by the prosperity of the disbelievers throughout the land. It is only a brief enjoyment. Then Hell will be their home— what an evil place to rest! [3:196-197]

ٱلَّذِينَ كَفَرُواْ وَصَدُّواْ عَن سَبِيلِ ٱللَّهِ أَضَلَّ أَعْمَـٰلَهُمْ ۝

Those who disbelieve and hinder from the Way of Allah, He will render their deeds void. [47:1]

إِنَّ ٱلَّذِينَ كَفَرُواْ يُنفِقُونَ أَمْوَٰلَهُمْ لِيَصُدُّواْ عَن سَبِيلِ ٱللَّهِ فَسَيُنفِقُونَهَا ثُمَّ تَكُونُ عَلَيْهِمْ حَسْرَةً ثُمَّ يُغْلَبُونَ وَٱلَّذِينَ كَفَرُوٓاْ إِلَىٰ جَهَنَّمَ يُحْشَرُونَ ۝

Surely the disbelievers spend their wealth to hinder others from the Path of Allah. They will continue to spend to the point of regret. Then they will be defeated and the disbelievers will be driven into Hell [8:36]

We cannot counter the sabotage and corruption of enemies of Islam without practicing Islam to its full extent, as individuals, families, and communities. This is the groundwork that must be laid first. Allah reminds us to stand tall, elevating our character and principles for His sake:

$$يَٰٓأَيُّهَا ٱلَّذِينَ ءَامَنُوٓاْ إِن تَنصُرُواْ ٱللَّهَ يَنصُرْكُمْ وَيُثَبِّتْ أَقْدَامَكُمْ ۝$$

O believers! If you stand up for Allah, He will help you and make your steps firm. [47:7]

$$وَلَيَنصُرَنَّ ٱللَّهُ مَن يَنصُرُهُۥٓ إِنَّ ٱللَّهَ لَقَوِىٌّ عَزِيزٌ ۝$$

Allah will certainly help those who stand up for Him. Allah is truly All-Powerful, Almighty. [22:40]

$$وَعَدَ ٱللَّهُ ٱلَّذِينَ ءَامَنُواْ مِنكُمْ وَعَمِلُواْ ٱلصَّٰلِحَٰتِ لَيَسْتَخْلِفَنَّهُمْ فِى ٱلْأَرْضِ كَمَا ٱسْتَخْلَفَ ٱلَّذِينَ مِن قَبْلِهِمْ وَلَيُمَكِّنَنَّ لَهُمْ دِينَهُمُ ٱلَّذِى ٱرْتَضَىٰ لَهُمْ وَلَيُبَدِّلَنَّهُم مِّنۢ بَعْدِ خَوْفِهِمْ أَمْنًا يَعْبُدُونَنِى لَا يُشْرِكُونَ بِى شَيْئًا ۝$$

Allah has promised those of you who believe and do good that He will certainly make them successors in the land, as He did with those before them; and will surely establish for them their faith which He has chosen for them; and will indeed change their fear into security, as they worship Me, associating nothing with Me. [24:55]

9. Disciplining the soul

Training ourselves in patience, consistency, and deliberation will prevent us from falling into the trap of haste. Patience, after all, only comes through practice, and whoever attempts to stay patient, then Allah will make him patient. This steady determination to attain a quality is the defining test of integrity.

10. Keeping the goal in mind

We as Muslims must always keep in mind our ultimate purpose in life. By focusing on the most pressing matters at hand and doing our best to perfect our actions, we will guard against becoming reactionary and disoriented. Only someone whose end goal is not clear to them will skip the preliminary matters as a shortcut.

11. Self-awareness and social awareness

Understanding the consequences of haste and impatience within and around us will lead to finding the most effective way to change it.

Deep understanding and knowledge drives away haste and immaturity in decision-making. Wisdom requires that we take all consequences into consideration, especially those in the long term.

The Methodology of Islamic Activism

Rash hastiness and impatience has no place in the correct approach to Islamic work. Our methodology for activism has been outlined and its boundaries have been set by revelation, the Prophet's example, and the arc of history. The journey seems long, but there is no other pathway forward.

On this path, the true heroes are those who practice perseverance, discipline, and consistent action. Whoever insists on enjoying the fruits of the harvest before they ripen, plucking the fragile blossoms before they have fruited, would be better off forgoing this mission for something else. But whoever can endure until the seed sprouts and the fruits fully ripen, then his or her reward with Allah lies in wait.

We must learn to balance between enthusiasm and intellect. Restrain the tide of your passions with the gravity of your thinking mind, but also allow your emotions to liven your logical processes. Let truth ground your imagination, but navigate reality in the glow of your dreams. Don't be distracted by every passing trend nor swat every fly you encounter, and do not swim against the tide of the laws of change. Use all of these forces to your advantage by redirecting them and engaging in one occasionally to ward off the other. Then await the hour of victory, for it lies just around the corner.

Dear reader, you seek God's pleasure and reward! These are guaranteed to you as long as you are sincerely devoted to them. God will not hold you accountable for the *results* of your actions, for He has only tasked you with being sincere in your actions and adequately prepared for the work. After we secure those two components, we will either fail and still receive the reward for our effort, or succeed while also securing the reward.

It has been proven time after time that this path of *dawah* and Islamic work is the greatest path of goodness. Do not be deterred by the labor required and do not speculate about when the end will come. Work while knowing that Allah is with you—He will not let your efforts go to waste. Success comes to those who work for it—Allah is too kind and compassionate to let you down!

Throughout our discussions so far on the various roadblocks in Islamic work, it appears that we must strive for the correct balance in our activism. We explored the dangers of spiritual burnout, which was a loss of momentum and halting after activity, and in this chapter, we discovered that going too fast is also a grave mistake. What is the right balance?

Teaching so wondrously through parables, the Quran draws our attention to the honeybee—one of Allah's creation that has so many lessons to teach us in our Islamic work. We can draw inspiration from the energy of the bees in their hives—not a single bee falls short in her duty to the hive, and not a single moment passes wherein her industrious buzzing fades.

At the same time, the bees are methodical and patient in awaiting results. The bees do not rush the product of their work, trusting the gradual process of nurturing a new generation and collecting and storing the nectar to create honey. The production of honey is a slow, collaborative process, often exceeding the lifespan of the bee who collected the initial drops of nectar. If any shortcuts were taken, this would disrupt the hive and result in its collapse.

Remember that there are levels and priorities to our work. Good ideas should be communicated, and good teachings should be spread with others. In order to be of value, speech should lead to action. Actions alone do not create change until there are those who are willing to sacrifice their time, wealth, and energy. This sacrifice is the greatest form of Islamic work, and it is necessary for our success as individuals and as an *ummah*.

> Ideas → Speech → Action → Sacrifice

Many people will talk. Not everyone who dreams of something will speak and advocate for it, but even fewer will roll up their sleeves and get to work. As the journey gets tough, even the action-oriented drop out, and the select few who stay the course are those with sincerity and grit. They are ready to strive deeply, work through callous conditions, and sacrifice. And even those few would burnout and break down if it wasn't for the help and support from Allah.

The story of Talut and his army is a beautiful illustration of the hierarchy of commitment among a society who all had high expectations for themselves. Everyone committed and gave lip service to the cause at first; but as events unfolded, some refused to follow the leader, others dropped out at the banks of the river, and the rest ran away when they saw the enemy. Only a small believing company remained, hands raised to the sky, appealing to Allah for help,

وَلَمَّا بَرَزُواْ لِجَالُوتَ وَجُنُودِهِۦ قَالُواْ رَبَّنَآ أَفْرِغْ عَلَيْنَا صَبْرًا وَثَبِّتْ أَقْدَامَنَا
وَٱنصُرْنَا عَلَى ٱلْقَوْمِ ٱلْكَٰفِرِينَ ۞

When they advanced to fight Goliath and his warriors they said,
"Our Lord! Shower us with perseverance, make our steps firm, and
give us victory over the disbelieving people." [2:250]

Prepare yourselves for the long road with a process of *tarbiyah* and test your resolve with consistent action. Wean yourself off of desires and petty preferences and accustom yourself to difficult, tiresome work. Do not let a moment pass without some good action coming out of it, for in that approach you will find the help and support of Allah.

✦ ✦ ✦

ENDNOTES

1. al-Bukhari, v. 4, p. 244
2. al-Bukhari, v. 3, p. 49, Muslim, #782
3. Muslim, #78, 79
4. al-Bukhari, v. 3, p. 182
5. al-Bukhari, v. 2, p. 179; Muslim, #1333
6. al-Bukhari, v. 2, p. 179, 180
7. al-Bukhari, v. 9, p. 59; Muslim, #1849
8. al-Bukhari, v. 9, p. 59, 60; Muslim, #1709
9. al-Minhāj: Sharh Ṣaḥeeḥ Muslim bin al-Hajjāj, v. 12, p. 229
10. Fath al-Bāri, v. 13, p. 8
11. al-Bukhari, v. 9, p. 80; Muslim, #142
12. Muslim, #290
13. al-Bukhari, v. 8, p. 38; Muslim #2998

Isolation

The words *'uzlah* and *tafarrud* have been used to describe a phenomenon of Muslims withdrawing from community and organized work due to a wide variety of excuses. *'Uzlah* is a distancing and withdrawal from something, while *tafarrud* is best translated as individualism.

Allah uses the former word when referring to the jinn and how they used to ascend into the sky to listen to the angels discussing matters of the unseen. When the revelation of the Quran to the Prophet ﷺ began, Allah used the shooting stars in the sky to drive the jinn away and isolate them from the heavenly realms, and so He says about them:

$$إِنَّهُمْ عَنِ ٱلسَّمْعِ لَمَعْزُولُونَ ۝$$

for <u>they are withdrawn</u> from overhearing. [26:212]

Allah uses the Arabic word *ma'zooloon*, which is derived from the same root as *'uzlah* (isolation) to describe how the jinn were physically cast away and removed from the sky.

Similarly, we use the same word to describe those who withdraw from the community, sparing themselves the burden of interaction and social responsibility. This is often done out of an idea that it is better to practice the spiritual aspects Islam without the distractions of social life. It may also be due to a lack of resilience in tolerating the burdens and headache of community work. A caller to Islam can also be afflicted by a mentality of individualism. Though they may be practicing Islam in the midst of others and even encourage others to grow in their faith, they only work on their own and steer away from joining with others.

> At our committee meeting at the mosque, our beloved Shaikh reminded us that "the hand of Allah is with the group." While used to hearing this reminder, I couldn't help but feel frustrated with group work. In an age where one can contribute with the click of a button, working within a masjid structure felt inefficient. I didn't want to wait around. I didn't want to have to trust people. In the mosque, we were trying to bring together Islamic workers who had completely different approaches—some had been volunteering for 30 years while others were new and excited to shake things up.
>
> Working on your own may seem more efficient and goal-oriented. And yet, the older I get, the more I realize that the process of doing collective work does a lot more for character growth than going at it alone. It takes a long time to turn a big boat. Sometimes the work becomes overwhelming, and we need to take a break from steering and become passengers. The dynamic of healthy group work requires knowing when to steer, maneuver, pull back and push forward.

Causes of Isolation

- A shallow understanding of Islam
- Misunderstood narratives of seclusion
- Ignorance of the Islamic balance
- Unrealistic expectations of community life
- Limited application of the concept of worship
- Being discouraged by widespread evil
- Misreading stories of sacrifice
- Friends who misguide
- Feeling overwhelmed by options for activism
- Underestimating the harms of isolation

A SHALLOW UNDERSTANDING OF ISLAM

Those who lack nuance and balance in understanding can easily fall in the trap of isolation and adopt an individualistic approach to community life. They may even cite scripture to support their choices. This indicates a shallow understanding of the Quran and Sunnah and a disregard for the abundant scriptural proofs highlighting the importance of societal life.

There are indeed some examples in our tradition that seem to encourage seclusion. The Prophet ﷺ said, for example,

> It will soon be so that the best property a Muslim has is some sheep that he follows around the peak of mountains or places of rainfall, fleeing from chaos with his religion.[1]

When someone asked, "Who is the most virtuous of all people?" the Messenger of Allah ﷺ responded, *"A man who strives in the path of Allah with his wealth and his life."* The man asked, "Then who?" He responded, *"A believer on one of the mountaintops who worships Allah —his Lord— and spares the people of his harm."*[2] The Prophet ﷺ once told Hudhayfah bin al-Yamān, *"Separate yourself from all of those sects, even if you must eat from the roots of trees, until death comes to you and you are in that state."*[3] In a riveting hadith, the Prophet ﷺ said,

> The best of lives for people are the following: a man who holds the reins of his horse for the sake of Allah, flying on its back. Every time he hears a battle cry or alarm, he flies to it, seeking to fight while expecting to die. Or it is a man among sheep on the peak of one of these mountaintops or at the basin of one of these valleys, who upholds the prayer, gives Zakah, and worships his Lord until death comes to him; there is nothing but good between him and others.[4]

As much as these texts appear to support isolation and withdrawal, they must be understood within context of all of Islam. Allah's commands in the Quran promote the vital importance of working together and contributing to society. This approach is at the heart of Islam, while seclusion is reserved for specific situations. Allah says,

وَتَعَاوَنُواْ عَلَى ٱلْبِرِّ وَٱلتَّقْوَىٰ ۖ وَلَا تَعَاوَنُواْ عَلَى ٱلْإِثْمِ وَٱلْعُدْوَٰنِ

*Cooperate with one another in goodness and righteousness, and do
not cooperate in sin and transgression.* [5:2]

وَٱعْتَصِمُواْ بِحَبْلِ ٱللَّهِ جَمِيعًا وَلَا تَفَرَّقُواْ

And hold firmly to the rope of Allah and do not be divided. [3:103]

إِنَّ ٱللَّهَ يُحِبُّ ٱلَّذِينَ يُقَٰتِلُونَ فِى سَبِيلِهِۦ صَفًّا كَأَنَّهُم بُنْيَٰنٌ مَّرْصُوصٌ ۝

*Surely Allah loves those who fight in His cause in ranks as if they
were one concrete structure.* [63:4]

Prophet Muhammad ﷺ emphasized the importance of working
together and staying close to the congregation of believers and the
Jama'ah, the mission-oriented community. He ﷺ said,

> Beware of division. Stay with the Jama'ah, for Satan is with
> the one who is alone, but further from the two who are
> together. Whoever wants the pinnacle of Paradise must stick
> to the Jama'ah.[5]

He also highlighted the power that comes with unity: *"The hand of
Allah is with the Jama'ah."*[6]

The Prophet ﷺ further emphasized the importance of holding to
the community and the mission when he said to his Companions,

> 'I instruct you with five things that Allah has instructed
> me with: the jama'ah, hearing and obeying, migration, and
> struggling in Allah's path. Whoever leaves the jama'ah by
> even the space of a handspan has stripped the knot of Islam
> from his neck until he returns....' They asked, 'Messenger of
> Allah, even if he fasts and prays?' He said, 'Even if he fasts,
> prays, and claims that he is a Muslim.'[7]

If we focus solely on the earlier group of texts that encourage solitude, neglecting to understand them in light of the wider concepts
of Islam, we will mistakenly assume isolation is a favorable option.
Such an approach is a selective reading of the scripture to serve our
own ends. Our religion is holistic in that it addresses the needs of
the individual while simultaneously developing a functioning and
righteous society. To neglect one of these goals would be an injustice
to Allah's religion and its objectives.

MISUNDERSTOOD NARRATIVES OF SECLUSION

There are several reports about Muslims in the early generations who chose a life of solitude. We can even see an example in the story of Prophet Abraham when he told his people,

وَأَعْتَزِلُكُمْ وَمَا تَدْعُونَ مِن دُونِ ٱللَّهِ

I shall distance myself from you all and from whatever you invoke besides Allah [19:48]

It would be foolish to neglect the events that drove Prophet Abraham to this measure. He had previously exerted all of his efforts and used every tool at his disposal in order to rectify his environment, but his people persisted in their delusional denial. It reached the point that he began to fear the effects on his own faith, and so he fled from his people.

There are also the examples of Abu Dharr, Ibn Umar, and some other Companions who isolated themselves from their communities in order to live alone during times of strife and confusion. The motivation for them to do so was to prevent themselves from having any share in the bloodshed that was occurring at the time. Those were times wherein the line between right and wrong was obscured by unprecedented chaos and ambiguity. Furthermore there is the example of Imam Mālik bin Anas, who was the head scholar in Madina during his time. He chose to isolate himself towards the end of his life in order to avoid the inevitable confrontation with the governing regime and to prevent bloodshed.

These great Companions and scholars contributed tremendously to the Muslim Ummah throughout their life, and their decision to opt for seclusion at a specific moment in their life was due to extenuating circumstances that were the exception rather than the rule. Someone who reads only a snapshot of the stories of leaders and scholars, without recognizing the context of their decisions, can mistakenly conclude that seclusion is the better option and find excuses to distance themselves from their communities.

Most people today are not seeking to avert a great tribulation when opting for seclusion, but rather are trying to avoid the headache of responsibility and exertion. If they were to dig deep into their motives, they would discover a self-centered interest that is antithetical to the approach of the role models they claim to follow.

Isolation or Loneliness

In our discussion of individualism, it's important to differentiate loneliness as a separate problem. Too many people in our community are lonely and suffer from lack of support, not by choice, but due to personal circumstance and shortcomings in the prevalent culture. Even if a person was convinced of the merits of community participation, they may not find it easy to find their place in community work and benefit from social support, even when they request it.

We must actively work to overcome this social disease of loneliness and imposed isolation by changing the culture of our communities, instituting healthy, inclusive social norms, and learning to be attentive and empathetic to others, especially the marginalized. In the culture of Islamic work, we must learn to emphasize inclusion and brotherhood, prioritizing it even over short-term results in our work. The Prophet ﷺ was brilliant in his approach to warding off loneliness in the hearts of his Companions, always sensitive to their inner condition and attentive to their needs. He made sure that every individual around him felt special and valued.

IGNORING THE ISLAMIC BALANCE

An individualistic Muslim may assume that if they were to commit to work within the community, they would lose their freedom. They imagine their personality being diluted and their strengths ignored when they are part of a team. This perceived loss of individuality is off-putting; they even fear that they, or their children, will lose the ability to distinguish between right and wrong due to social pressures. These assumptions are rooted in an ignorance of Islam's prescription of balance between the individual and the society.

Islam calls upon the individual to live in the midst of a community and find comfort in its shade. At the same time, each person is responsible for their own individual actions. Allah says,

وَلَا تَزِرُ وَازِرَةٌ وِزْرَ أُخْرَىٰ ۚ وَإِن تَدْعُ مُثْقَلَةٌ إِلَىٰ حِمْلِهَا لَا يُحْمَلْ مِنْهُ شَىْءٌ

وَلَوۡ كَانَ ذَا قُرۡبَىٰٓ

*No soul burdened with sin will bear the burden of another. And if
a sin-burdened soul cries for help with its burden, none of it will be
carried—even by a close relative. [35:18]*

كُلُّ نَفۡسٍۭ بِمَا كَسَبَتۡ رَهِينَةٌ

Every soul will be detained for what it has done [74:38]

وَٱتَّقُوا۟ يَوۡمًا لَّا تَجۡزِى نَفۡسٌ عَن نَّفۡسٍ شَيۡـًٔا

*Guard yourselves against the Day no soul will be of help to another
[2:48]*

بَلِ ٱلۡإِنسَٰنُ عَلَىٰ نَفۡسِهِۦ بَصِيرَةٌ ۝ وَلَوۡ أَلۡقَىٰ مَعَاذِيرَهُۥ ۝

*In fact, people will testify against their own souls, despite the
excuses they come up with. [5:14-15]*

Islam balances this individual accountability with responsibility
toward the collective; each person must do his or her best to support, empower, and advise fellow Muslims.

﴾ نصيحة ﴿

Naṣeeḥah: sincerity, advice and counsel. Encompasses
many meanings, the common thread being sincerely wishing well for others.

The Prophet ﷺ said, *"The religion is naseehah."* His companions
responded to this statement by asking, *"To whom?"* He said, *"To
Allah, to His scripture, to the leaders of the Muslims, and to the
general populace."*[8]
There is no better living example of commitment to community
development than the Prophet ﷺ himself. He devoted his life to
helping others in their worldly and spiritual matters, and he was
known as the person to go to when help was needed. This empathy
and consideration is patently evident in his instructions to his Companions, as he would often clarify for them the importance of collective effort.
Prophet Muhammad ﷺ said, *"The believer is a mirror for his
fellow believer, and a believer is a brother to his fellow believer. He*

prevents him from loss and guards his back." In another wording, he said, *"The believer is his brother's mirror. If he sees a flaw in him, he corrects it."*[9]

The Companions lived alongside the Prophet ﷺ in a community; they did not lose their individual personalities and idiosyncrasies, nor did any of their brilliance fade in light of the others. They counseled, sought advice, and encouraged each other to do good while preventing each other from evil. One Companion even told Umar, whose reputation for being quick to anger was not lost on any of them: "If we see any crookedness in you, we will straighten it with our swords!"

Through organized, collective Islamic work and a methodology of tarbiyah, the Muslim individual is balanced and developed in a most exceptional way. His or her awareness of the environment is heightened, guarding against weakness, while his or her brothers and sisters alert each other to flaws and potential missteps. Neglecting these communal tenets of Islam can lead individuals to cling to a false sense of safety in isolation, while in reality they have placed themselves in a position of vulnerability.

UNREALISTIC EXPECTATIONS OF COMMUNITY LIFE

Some are driven to withdraw from the community or Islamic work after becoming disillusioned by negative experiences. There are many beautiful and uplifting aspects of community life, but there is also disappointment and annoyance. Being part of a group can be tedious and even painful at times. The Muslim, especially the activist and volunteer who works for the sake of Allah, should adjust their expectations accordingly. Sharing our life and working side by side with the community entails enduring hardship and inconvenience for the sake of others. We may be called upon to perform tedious chores and unwelcome tasks, stretching ourselves thin and compensating for the shortcomings of others.

Part of the development of the Islamic worker is coming to terms with the realities of being at the service of the community and working as a team. Through this humbling process of tarbiyah, the soul is developed and disciplined. We should not allow our personal comfort and preferences stand in the way of the immense reward and character refinement that comes with enduring discomfort for the sake of the community. Without realistic expectations and a willingness to put up with hardship, the individual will be easily demoralized by the path of Islamic work and community life, having no choice but to resort to a less rewarding, isolated existence.

When Community Politics Drives People Away

Community politics and ethnic-based tribalism in many of our spaces drive many people away from Islamic work. Expecting to find Islamic values of inclusion, tolerance, and empowerment practiced in our communities, eager newcomers to Islamic work are disillusioned upon finding inhospitable, exclusionary environments and may drop out completely from Islamic activism.

In order to empower healthy Islamic work and social bonds, it is important to work together to build communities based on true Islamic principles and address the different ailments faced by Muslims. There is an individual dimension to enacting this change—a positive attitude, willingness to tolerate discomfort for the sake of the group, assuming the best of others, and appreciating a gradual approach to change. There is also a communal dimension falling squarely on the shoulders of community insiders who hold influence to lead the way to change in their communities. If such change is not enacted, the community becomes stagnant and eventually irrelevant for a growing segment of individuals it ought to serve.

MISUNDERSTANDING THE CONCEPT OF WORSHIP IN ISLAM

Many who fall into the trap of individualism submit the excuse that social interactions take time and attention away from worshipping Allah. Rather than visit a friend or host guests, they would prefer to spend their time in prayer, fasting, reciting the Quran, and other noble acts of worship.

Anyone who offers such an excuse for isolating themselves from others is gravely mistaken in their understanding of worship. Ibn Taymiyah clarifies this succinctly, defining worship as a comprehensive term for everything Allah loves and is pleased with, encompassing speech and actions, outward and inward. Ibn Taymiyah continues:

Prayer, zakah, fasting, and hajj are worship, as are *dua'*, words of forgiveness, remembrance, and reciting Quran. Telling the truth, fulfilling trusts, honoring one's parents, and keeping good relations with relatives are worship. Fulfilling a promise is worship, and inviting to good is worship. Encouraging the good, forbidding evil, and fighting against disbelief and hypocrisy is worship.

Caring for one's neighbor and being kind towards the orphan, the needy, the traveler and the servant are acts of worship. Being merciful with the weak and gentle with animals is an act of worship. Love of Allah and His Messenger, humility before God, repenting to Him, sincerity, patience with God's will, accepting His decree, relying upon Him, hoping in His mercy and fearing His punishment, and so on, all fall under worship.

Many of the above-mentioned elements involve a high level of social engagement, but are still ranked as acts of worship. We find this confirmed all throughout the Quran and the example of the Prophet ﷺ.

Interaction with others does not mean we should not set aside time for solitary worship. We can make time in our schedules to come closer to Allah through remembrance, learning, recitation, and reflection. This is why Umar bin al-Khattab said, "Take your share of seclusion." However, anyone who attempts to justify their withdrawal from the community and the arena of organized work by stressing their need to "worship" does not understand what worship is.

Worship is such a comprehensive and versatile concept in Islam, encompassing the individual and the collective, remembrance and service, gratitude and work. To limit it strictly to the ritual is a gross misunderstanding and injustice to the religion. One who fails to understand the definition of worship will be under the illusion that community engagement is an obstacle to worship, when in fact it is part and parcel of worship and service to Allah.

BEING INTIMIDATED BY WIDESPREAD EVIL

If someone doesn't know what the Muslim's role should be during times of widespread corruption, their fear could lead them to isolation. A Muslim should be energetic and proactive in rectifying the world, even amidst dark and demoralizing conditions. Fleeing into seclusion is an extreme measure only to be taken in rare circumstances when no other options are available to the Muslim community.

When those working for Islam do not prioritize positive action and consistent service, pessimism will be the prevalent mood. We must be willing to withstand the bleak situation, fighting against evil and injustice with every ounce of strength in our bones. If we all choose solitude over resistance, comfort over sacrifice, the world would be a much more dismal place than it already is. Allah says,

$$ وَلَوْلَا دَفْعُ ٱللَّهِ ٱلنَّاسَ بَعْضَهُم بِبَعْضٍ لَّفَسَدَتِ ٱلْأَرْضُ $$

Had Allah not repelled a group of people by another, corruption would have dominated the earth [2:251]

He also said,

$$ وَلَوْلَا دَفْعُ ٱللَّهِ ٱلنَّاسَ بَعْضَهُم بِبَعْضٍ لَّهُدِّمَتْ صَوَامِعُ وَبِيَعٌ وَصَلَوَاتٌ وَمَسَاجِدُ يُذْكَرُ فِيهَا ٱسْمُ ٱللَّهِ كَثِيرًا $$

Had Allah not repelled some people by means of others, destruction would have surely destroyed monasteries, churches, synagogues, and mosques in which Allah's Name is often mentioned. [22:40]

It also serves well to mention again the hadith discussed earlier in the chapter, in which the Prophet ﷺ said,

> The one who upholds Allah's boundaries and the one who crosses them are like a group of people who drew lots on a ship. Some received the upper deck while the others received the lower deck. Whenever the ones in the lower deck would take water to drink, they would pass by the ones on the upper deck, so they said, "We should just poke a hole for ourselves so as not to bother those above us." If they allowed them to do this, then they would all perish, but if they held their hands back, they would all be safe together.[10]

MISREADING STORIES OF SACRIFICE

While many Muslims are inspired by those scholars, leaders, and activists who endured hardship and torture for the cause of Islam, some individuals may react with fear. They caution their loved ones from taking the path of Islamic work lest they fall into similar circumstances. One may also think that they could never withstand such trials, therefore it would be better to leave Islamic work to those who are stronger.

But the torture and hardship is only one side of the story—it is important to see the great reward, honor, and rank assigned to such people. These heroic men and women who suffered at the hands of unjust and evil powers had reached a high level of certainty in their faith, a certainty which can transform suffering into contentment. Allah made them firm in their stance against evil and ultimately granted them victory:

وَكَأَيِّن مِّن نَّبِيٍّ قَٰتَلَ مَعَهُ رِبِّيُّونَ كَثِيرٌ فَمَا وَهَنُوا لِمَا أَصَابَهُمْ فِى سَبِيلِ ٱللَّهِ وَمَا ضَعُفُوا وَمَا ٱسْتَكَانُوا وَٱللَّهُ يُحِبُّ ٱلصَّٰبِرِينَ ۝ وَمَا كَانَ قَوْلَهُمْ إِلَّا أَن قَالُوا رَبَّنَا ٱغْفِرْ لَنَا ذُنُوبَنَا وَإِسْرَافَنَا فِى أَمْرِنَا وَثَبِّتْ أَقْدَامَنَا وَٱنصُرْنَا عَلَى ٱلْقَوْمِ ٱلْكَٰفِرِينَ ۝ فَـَٔاتَىٰهُمُ ٱللَّهُ ثَوَابَ ٱلدُّنْيَا وَحُسْنَ ثَوَابِ ٱلْآخِرَةِ وَٱللَّهُ يُحِبُّ ٱلْمُحْسِنِينَ ۝

Consider how many devotees fought along with their prophets and never faltered despite whatever they suffered in the cause of Allah, nor did they weaken or give in! Allah loves those who persevere. And all they said was, "Our Lord! Forgive our sins and excesses, make our steps firm, and grant us victory over the disbelieving people." So Allah gave them the reward of this world and the excellent reward of the Hereafter, for Allah loves the good-doers. [3:146-148]

It can be intimidating to hear about the instances wherein the righteous were being slain and tortured, without understanding the level of faith and certainty they had reached before their test. It is important to emphasize the strong faith and the shining light in the hearts of such figures. Allah never tests a person until they are ready to bear the weight of the test. It is also important to keep in mind the other half of the equation—the reward of the hereafter which will make the pain and suffering in this life fade entirely.

FRIENDS WHO MISLEAD

Having friends who are overly critical of Islamic work, averse to community engagement, and who cater to their own comfort instead of the collective good can cause us to adopt similar attitudes. Public critiques of community work and Islamic organizations may seem clever and discerning, but what beneficial fruits have those critiques reaped?

We are heavily influenced by those with whom we spend our time. Their attitudes and life choices easily rub off on us, including the social media feeds and accounts that we subscribe to. This is why the Prophet ﷺ said, *"A person is upon the religion of his closest friend, so look at who you take as a close friend."*[11]

FEELING OVERWHELMED BY OPTIONS FOR ACTIVISM

The large number of groups and organizations dedicated to Islamic work can seem exhausting to someone who is figuring out where they should apply their efforts. We often don't know whom we should work with and whom we should avoid. Making a choice seems too much of a commitment, so some opt to remain noncommittal.

It is important to realize that the majority of these institutions are good, albeit at varying degrees. We must get to know them all and choose the organization with the most good to offer. At the end of this chapter, the author identifies some key qualities to keep an eye out for when searching for the ideal organization or group to work with.

UNDERESTIMATING THE HARMS OF ISOLATION

The effects of individualism and isolation are detrimental to both the individual and to the momentum of Islamic work, but many people are unaware of this; perhaps they even think their isolation is piety. We must educate ourselves and others about these harms as a deterrent against the disease of individualism and isolation.

Effects of Isolation

Opting to set oneself apart from the community has many harmful consequences on one's own spiritual work, as well as on the field of Islamic work as a whole. The effects on the individual and community include the following:

- Untapped potential
- Lack of mentorship
- Stunted development
- Missing out on second-hand experiences
- Overwhelming despair
- Missing out on reward
- Inability to establish Islam in themselves or others
- Being subject to sin
- Vulnerability to defeat
- Disqualifying from Allah's help

UNTAPPED POTENTIAL

No matter how smart or intelligent you might be, there is no way to know the extent of your own potential in solitude. We require others to extract that potential. We need to engage consistently with people before we can know whether our dominant characteristics are harsh, selfish, generous or empathetic. Our potential for patience is another good example of this; we cannot know how tolerant we are until we interact with others and observe whether we react to their flaws with forbearance.

Social Situations Shed Light on Character

Self-awareness plays such a crucial role in our personal development; this includes awareness of our tendencies in social situations. Working closely with others and exposing ourselves to different social situations shed light on our flaws and strengths. Many young people discover aspects of their personalities they may not have known upon major life transitions such as having kids and getting married. Certain situations bring out the absolute best in us, while others can do the opposite —we should use both experiences to improve our character. Sticking with the community, learning how to work in a team, and developing resilience in social relationships can be an invaluable form of tarbiyah (self-development and character building).

We can assess our own courage and allegiance to the truth by observing how we deal with those who err in front of us. Can we overcome our fear of discomfort in order to speak out and correct wrongdoing? Interacting with others is the ultimate test of our own honesty and trustworthiness. Such character qualities can only be exercised in a group setting; you cannot be truthful if you rarely speak with people, and you cannot be trustworthy if there is no one to keep your promises to. This is perhaps what the Prophet ﷺ meant when he said, *"One believer is a mirror to another."*[12] Umar is also quoted to have said, "May Allah show mercy to anyone who points out our flaws to us."[13]

To live in seclusion is to live in blindness. How amazing it is that God made joining hands with the community and collaboration the best way to exercise our character and discover our own selves! Moreover, the mission as a whole benefits when individuals reach their potential and strengthen their resilience and character. We can see how a mission-driven community empowers and develops its members to improve, and in turn those individuals strengthen the collective.

When a Muslim lives in seclusion, he or she never discovers their own potential for good, and this is truly a loss. Their lack of knowledge and consultation with righteous peers might lead them to do evil while thinking that it is good, or to leave off an act of good, thinking that it is evil.

قُلْ هَلْ نُنَبِّئُكُم بِٱلْأَخْسَرِينَ أَعْمَلًا ۝ ٱلَّذِينَ ضَلَّ سَعْيُهُمْ فِى ٱلْحَيَوٰةِ ٱلدُّنْيَا وَهُمْ يَحْسَبُونَ أَنَّهُمْ يُحْسِنُونَ صُنْعًا ۝

Say, "Shall we inform you of who will lose the most deeds? They are those whose efforts are in vain in this worldly life, while they think they are doing good!" [18:103-104]

LACK OF MENTORSHIP

Living in seclusion deprives one of the opportunity for mentorship. In our communities, there are individuals who are ready to take others by the hand and cultivate them—we will not find those mentors, nor they us, unless we enter the field of collective work. Even if we are aware of our own flaws and shortcomings, we might not take the best action to correct them without some form of accountability—a mentor can provide that extra push. A life of isolation strips us of the chance to spend time with mentors who can help us overcome our own egos and steadily improve character and spirituality.

This is why the Prophet ﷺ so often stressed the importance of having friends who make us better Muslims. He said, *"The believer is his brother's mirror. Whenever he sees a flaw in him, he corrects it."*[14] He also said,

> When Allah wants good for someone to whom he gives leadership over the affairs of the Muslims, He gives him an advisor of truth. When he forgets, [the advisor] reminds him, and when he remembers, [the advisor] assists him.[15]

STUNTED DEVELOPMENT

An individualistic attitude makes us easy prey for Satan. The human being is a complex creature, made up of a physical and a spiritual essence. The soul is made up of qualities and instincts that are intricately woven together with their opposites; each pair runs adjacent but in opposite directions. These include such instincts as fear and hope, love and hate, pragmatism and imagination, physical and emotional senses, and all of the other contradictory but complementary forces within us. Like the opposite ends of pillars upon which a structure rests, each of these is vital to our human composition. The only true way to strike a complete balance in life is to give each of these their due right.

A mission-driven community is the ideal environment in which we employ all of these components to equal degrees, in tandem with one another. It is where we realize our greatest potential, while developing a balanced, resilient personality. Through mission-driven teamwork and community, we eliminate many of the deficiencies of our character, leaving little room for Satan's subtle incitements to evil. When a Muslim distances himself from the community and chooses to focus solely on his individual needs, he stunts the growth of some of those components, leaving gaps in his foundation for Satan to settle in. This is likely what the Prophet ﷺ was drawing our attention to when he said,

Whoever among you would like the peak of Paradise must then stick to the jama'ah, for Satan is with the one who is alone, but further from the two who are together."[16]

MISSING OUT ON SECOND-HAND EXPERIENCE

Living in isolation deprives us of the opportunity to benefit and learn from the experiences of others. These relationships can help us navigate new situations; we can apply wisdom gained from those who tread this path before us. The path of working for God's religion is fraught with sacrifice and difficulty, and learning how to navigate it from other sensible, intelligent Muslim activists can help us overcome the challenges we are bound to face.

When someone dismisses mission-driven community work, he or she misses out on benefitting from these valuable insights. Their perspective will remain narrow and short-sighted for as long as they limit themselves to their own experience. No light of perspective and advice will illuminate their paths; instead they will suffer alone and be forced to overcome challenges alone.

The Prophet ﷺ alluded to the benefits of companionship in his teachings. In the hadith mentioned earlier, he compared a good friend to a perfume seller who, *"will either offer you some perfume free of charge, or you will buy some from him, or you will smell from him a pleasant fragrance."* The lessons and experiences we can gain from good company can allow us to rejuvenate ourselves and enhance our journey to pleasing Allah.

OVERWHELMING DESPAIR

From time to time, Satan casts doubts into the minds of everyone working for Islam about the work that they do. He tries to convince them that it is not worth all of the trouble to continue this work—there is so little progress while there is so much suffering. He whispers that the enemies of Islam are simply too powerful, so it is better to just save yourself by retreating to the sidelines. These whispers are easy to repel in the companionship of brothers and sisters who raise each other up and urge you to keep going, reminding you of the nobility of your cause. Interacting on a regular basis with people who share your objectives, values, and concerns will motivate you to keep on despite the challenges and unfavorable circumstances.

Someone who is pursuing a lofty objective, but working toward it on their own, can easily succumb to these doubts that only continue to grow with time. They have no one to reassure them and help repel this feeling of inadequacy, and such feelings may overwhelm them to the point of hopelessness. More likely than not, this lone traveler will end up pulling over to the side of the road, falling short in their duty to Allah's religion due to burnout and frustration.

MISSING OUT ON REWARD

Someone who lives with others and interacts with them encounters many more opportunities for reward than someone who lives distanced from the community. There are gatherings wherein they can either learn or teach, sick people whom they can visit, occasions of joy and sorrow which they can share or offer comfort, efforts they can contribute to, and brothers and sisters whom they can support and remember Allah with. While someone who lives amidst others is accumulating rewards for these small and grand deeds of kindness, the reward of someone who lives in seclusion remains limited.

INABILITY TO ESTABLISH ISLAM IN THEMSELVES OR OTHERS

Falsehood never stops spreading for a single moment on earth. Its objective is to transform this world into the greatest extremes of evil and corruption. The only way falsehood could ever reach that point is if the people who are supposed to stand for the truth give up on their mission or become too scattered and self-concerned to put up a fight. A Muslim who flees from society has fled from the battle altogether, splintering off from the main body of resistance to attempt a feeble individual contribution. Such a person has not only abandoned his fellow Muslims at a time of desperate need, but has also drained his own chances of success.

Allah alludes to this in the Quran. Highlighting the importance of resisting the force of falsehood, He says,

وَلَوْلَا دَفْعُ ٱللَّهِ ٱلنَّاسَ بَعْضَهُم بِبَعْضٍ لَّفَسَدَتِ ٱلْأَرْضُ

*Had Allah not repelled a group of people by another, corruption
would have dominated the earth...* [2:251]

He also says,

وَلَوْلَا دَفْعُ ٱللَّهِ ٱلنَّاسَ بَعْضَهُم بِبَعْضٍ لَّهُدِّمَتْ صَوَامِعُ وَبِيَعٌ وَصَلَوَٰتٌ
وَمَسَٰجِدُ يُذْكَرُ فِيهَا ٱسْمُ ٱللَّهِ كَثِيرًا وَلَيَنصُرَنَّ ٱللَّهُ مَن يَنصُرُهُۥ إِنَّ ٱللَّهَ
لَقَوِيٌّ عَزِيزٌ ۞

*Had Allah not repelled some people by means of others, destruction
would have surely claimed monasteries, churches, synagogues,
and mosques in which Allah's Name is often mentioned. Allah
will certainly help those who stand up for Him. Allah is truly All-
Powerful, Almighty.* [22:40]

The Messenger of Allah ﷺ further emphasized this when he said,

> The one who upholds Allah's boundaries and the one who
> crosses them are like a group of people who drew lots on a
> ship. Some received the upper deck while the others received
> the lower deck. Whenever the ones in the lower deck would
> take water to drink, they would pass by the ones on the
> upper deck, so they said, 'We should just poke a hole for
> ourselves so as not to bother those above us." If they allow
> them to do this, then they will all perish, but if they held
> their hands back, they would all be safe together.'[17]

BEING SUBJECT TO SIN

Leaving society and abandoning collective, mission-driven work can
put someone at risk of sinning and earning God's displeasure. How
can a Muslim even begin to accept that for themselves? Allah says,

وَمَن يَحْلِلْ عَلَيْهِ غَضَبِي فَقَدْ هَوَىٰ ۞

Whomever My wrath befalls is certainly doomed. [20:81]

The Prophet ﷺ also warned against this grave risk. He said, "*Whoever breaks obedience and separates himself from the community
and then dies has died a death of Jahiliyah (ignorance).*"[18]

VULNERABILITY TO DEFEAT

It is important to realize that the decision to isolate oneself and focus on personal interests does not just impact an individual, but affects the community as a whole. By losing one member, a team is more vulnerable. The burden of sustaining the work is now shared by less people, so it takes a longer time and more strenuous effort in order to produce results. This is true of any organization whose members are scattered and disunified.

It is no wonder, then, that the enemies of Allah are so keen on keeping Muslims divided. They are following the commonly employed strategy of "divide and conquer." Conversely, we can also understand why Allah commands us to stay united upon His cause and warns us against infighting. He says,

وَٱعْتَصِمُوا بِحَبْلِ ٱللَّهِ جَمِيعًا وَلَا تَفَرَّقُوا

And hold firmly to the rope of Allah and do not be divided. [3:103]

He also says,

وَأَطِيعُوا ٱللَّهَ وَرَسُولَهُ وَلَا تَنَازَعُوا فَتَفْشَلُوا وَتَذْهَبَ رِيحُكُمْ

Obey Allah and His Messenger and do not dispute with one another,
or you would be discouraged and weakened. [8:46]

And He says,

وَتَعَاوَنُوا عَلَى ٱلْبِرِّ وَٱلتَّقْوَىٰ وَلَا تَعَاوَنُوا عَلَى ٱلْإِثْمِ وَٱلْعُدْوَٰنِ

Cooperate with one another in goodness and righteousness, and do
not cooperate in sin and transgression. [5:2]

DISQUALIFYING FROM ALLAH'S HELP

The Islamic movement, no matter how capable and vast in numbers, will always require the help of Allah in order to succeed. Allah promised that He would not grant His divine assistance to us unless we are working together, side by side. This is why the Prophet ﷺ said, *"The hand of Allah is with the jama'ah."*[19]

Being deprived of this divine aid is indeed a test and trial for the community. Those who remain steadfast and patient in the arena of Islamic work despite deadlock and obstacles will only be increased in their reward and blessings—for them, the delay of success is a mercy and a raising of rank. On the other hand, those who isolate themselves and choose to go it alone will be contributing to the suffering of the community and be deserving of punishment. Allah says,

$$\text{وَٱلَّذِينَ قُتِلُوا۟ فِى سَبِيلِ ٱللَّهِ فَلَن يُضِلَّ أَعْمَٰلَهُمْ ۝ سَيَهْدِيهِمْ وَيُصْلِحُ بَالَهُمْ ۝ وَيُدْخِلُهُمُ ٱلْجَنَّةَ عَرَّفَهَا لَهُمْ ۝}$$

And those who are martyred in the cause of Allah, He will never render their deeds void. He will guide them, improve their condition, and admit them into Paradise, having made it known to them. [47:4-6]

This is also echoed in the Prophet's ﷺ words,

> Whenever Allah sends a punishment down to a people, the punishment reaches whoever is among them. Then they are resurrected based on their deeds.[20]

These are the most important individual and communal consequences of isolation that we must beware of. They can all be understood in light of the Prophet's ﷺ word of caution: *"Whoever leaves the jama'ah by even the space of a handspan has stripped the knot of Islam from his neck..."*[21] We can understand from this that whoever departs from the mission-driven community on a matter that is agreed upon has subjected themselves to loss and destruction. The metaphor is apt, as he compared anyone who does so to a camel or horse who slips off the knot of the rope that keeps them in place. By doing so, they can run off in any direction, only to be found later having fallen victim to hunger or wild predators.

Remedies for Isolation

Now that we have discussed the causes that drive people into isolation and the harmful effects that it has on the individual and the collective Islamic movement, we can turn our attention to the ways of avoiding this roadblock. Some of the most powerful remedies for isolation and an individualistic mindset are:

- A holistic understanding of Islam
- Putting seclusion in its proper context
- Understanding self-development in light of community
- Correct understanding of worship
- Constant self-assessment
- Understanding a Muslim's duty amidst widespread evil
- A complete return to Allah
- Avoiding those who are negative
- Understanding the realities of Islamic organizations
- Following the footsteps of Allah's Messenger ﷺ
- Realizing the looming threat
- Taking note of the natural world around us
- Realizing the harms of an individualistic culture

1. A holistic understanding of Islam

There are numerous examples throughout the Quran and Sunnah that encourage social engagement, and a few that encourage seclusion. These must be understood in light of one another and in context of the religion as a whole. Understanding them correctly will drive any Muslim who is truthful and sincere in their practice of the religion to avoid such seclusion and to be part and parcel of their community. Examining the Quran, the hadith, and the life of the Prophet ﷺ helps us realize that Muslims are expected to engage with their communities by default, and seclusion is an extreme measure to be taken only when our faith or our lives are in emminent danger.

2. Putting seclusion in its proper context

Likewise, there are many stories of some of the most righteous and exemplary Muslims who adopted an extreme measure of seclusion, especially in the early history of Islam. Understanding the circumstances that led them to make those decisions will prevent us from thinking that seclusion in our context would be justified.

Because there was an official Islamic governing body that maintained the necessary institutions required to sustain the practice of the religion, an individual was able to withdraw from the public lens without compromising the communal practice of religion. If we, on the other hand, secluded ourselves, the harmful consequences that were previously discussed at length would render us liable for the weakened state of Islam in our world.

3. Understanding self-development in light of community

The Islamic approach to self-development aims not only to improve the individual, but improve society through the individual. Following this approach is sure to introduce a positive, proactive spirit in the Muslim community. By bettering the community, we better ourselves in the process. It also ensures that our own individuality and social and emotional needs are simultaneously preserved.

4. A correct understanding of worship

Knowing that the correct implementation of worship goes beyond the ritual acts like prayer and fasting will safeguard us against an individualistic approach. Understanding worship through this holistic lens abolishes a false dichotomy of ritual and community life. It helps us perceive the importance of staying within a community and engaging with others as instrumental to our own practice of Islam. We will begin to value participation in social events and interacting with others, without mistakenly assuming that it is taking away from our spirituality.

5. Constant self-assessment

We must always be on guard against our own souls, holding ourselves to firm standards and monitoring our behavior and urges. Otherwise, our passions will take control, and our desires will defeat us. When we are self-aware, we will recognize the selfish impulses that lure us to retreat from Islamic work and community efforts and take the proper action to counter them.

6. Understanding a Muslim's duty in times of widespread evil

When evil and corruption are on the rise, it is the Muslim's duty to counter it with righteousness. Knowing the importance of this role is enough to bring any individualistic individual out of their isolation, forcing them to work with others in order to repel evil. We must be vigilant against the spread of evil and proactive in fulfilling our duty to our communities, as we will be asked in the hereafter about what we did.

7. A complete return to Allah

We can prevent ourselves from falling into the trap of isolation by sincerely asking Allah for help. He will never turn down anyone who knocks on His door. He says,

$$وَإِذَا سَأَلَكَ عِبَادِى عَنِّى فَإِنِّى قَرِيبٌ ۖ أُجِيبُ دَعْوَةَ ٱلدَّاعِ إِذَا دَعَانِ ۖ فَلْيَسْتَجِيبُوا۟ لِى وَلْيُؤْمِنُوا۟ بِى لَعَلَّهُمْ يَرْشُدُونَ$$

When My servants ask you about Me: I am truly near. I respond to one's prayer when they call upon Me. So let them respond to Me and believe in Me, perhaps they will be guided. [2:186]

8. Avoiding those who are negative

We must not take as close friends those who lack the proper understanding of the aforementioned concepts. Their negativity may encourage us to withdraw from the community or give up hope. They might promote or even practice such extreme understandings of seclusion, influencing us to do the same. Avoiding their prolonged company will protect us from falling into the same trap.

9. Understanding the realities of Islamic organizations

Numerous Islamic organizations around us all claim to work for good, even though they may fail to actualize much in reality. This may be due to either incompetence or ill will. In any case, it is important for us to familiarize ourselves with each organization and assess them according to the aforementioned guidelines in order to determine which ones we should or should not work with. Choosing the right institutions to be a part of can definitely save someone from falling into the trap of seclusion, sparing them some of the bitter encounters others have experienced. At the end of this chapter are some guidelines on choosing groups and organizations to work with.

10. Studying how the Prophet ﷺ bolstered Islamic identity

The Prophet ﷺ exerted his efforts in constructing the image of strength and honor for the Muslim community early on. There were many organizational and institutional aspects of the community that he ﷺ established in Medina to keep the diverse community engaged and unified. Doing this for our communities can save many from isolating themselves from the rest of the group, as Allah has promised us that following His Messenger's ﷺ example in all facets of life brings nothing but good:

$$لَّقَدۡ كَانَ لَكُمۡ فِى رَسُولِ ٱللَّهِ أُسۡوَةٌ حَسَنَةٌ لِّمَن كَانَ يَرۡجُوا۟ ٱللَّهَ وَٱلۡيَوۡمَ ٱلۡءَاخِرَ وَذَكَرَ ٱللَّهَ كَثِيرًا ۝$$

Indeed, in the Messenger of Allah you have an excellent example for whoever has hope in Allah and the Last Day, and remembers Allah often. [33:21]

11. Realizing the looming threat

The enemies of Allah —both the explicit rejectors of Islam and the hypocrites who feign belief— are working together to defeat Islam. They work day and night, and they move in unison despite their many differences. Yet the Muslims still drive wedges between one another over inconsequential disagreements, preventing us from being able to come together to defend Islam against its enemies. Allah makes this clear to us, leaving no room for isolation from the Muslim community:

$$وَٱلَّذِينَ كَفَرُوا۟ بَعۡضُهُمۡ أَوۡلِيَآءُ بَعۡضٍ إِلَّا تَفۡعَلُوهُ تَكُن فِتۡنَةٌ فِى ٱلۡأَرۡضِ وَفَسَادٌ كَبِيرٌ$$

As for the disbelievers, they are guardians of one another. And unless you act likewise, there will be great oppression and corruption in the land. [8:73]

12. Taking note of the natural world around us

Reflecting on how the creatures on earth operate and how the universe itself is designed leads us to the realization that there is nothing that thrives in seclusion. All living organisms participate in some form of community, cooperating in order to fulfill their individual roles therein. Consider how bees support one another: some build, some cleanse, some nurture, some protect, and some go out in order to bring back the nectar. All of these processes are necessary to produce honey. The same observations can be made for how ants build their colonies, how birds migrate, and even how the rays of the sun reach the earth to provide warmth and light.

Collaboration and cooperation are essential components of survival and progress. If creatures with no sense of intellect internalize the necessity of teamwork, how are we so blind and neglectful of it? Staying mindful and observant of this reality can help us avoid the trap of self-centered seclusion and uphold our duties to our communities.

13. Realizing the harms of an individualistic culture

Acknowledging the extent to which seclusion harms the individual and society is vital in preventing us from succumbing to it. The consequences are numerous and far-reaching in their impact. Any sensible person would see the dangers of isolation and understand the need to stay away from it.

Choosing the Right Group

Some people may feel overwhelmed by the many organizations and groups on the Islamic work scene. Instead of reacting with confusion, it is helpful to see the existence of many groups and organizations working to further the goals of Islam as the sign of an energetic community and an Islamic movement that is growing. As we consider which groups to join or support, we should examine them carefully and ask a number of questions.

✓ *Is the group's ultimate goal to practice Allah's laws?*

Allah says,

$$\text{إِنِ ٱلْحُكْمُ إِلَّا لِلَّهِ}$$

It is only Allah Who presides. [6:57]

$$\text{وَأَنِ ٱحْكُم بَيْنَهُم بِمَآ أَنزَلَ ٱللَّهُ}$$

And judge between them by what Allah has revealed... [5:49]

✓ *Do the actions and decisions of the organization or group seek out Allah's pleasure above all else?*

$$\text{قُلْ إِنَّ صَلَاتِى وَنُسُكِى وَمَحْيَاىَ وَمَمَاتِى لِلَّهِ رَبِّ ٱلْعَٰلَمِينَ ۝ لَا}$$

شَرِيكَ لَهُ وَبِذَٰلِكَ أُمِرْتُ وَأَنَا أَوَّلُ ٱلْمُسْلِمِينَ ۝

Say, "Surely my prayer, my worship, my life, and my death are
all for Allah—Lord of all worlds. He has no partner. So I am
commanded, and so I am the first to submit." [6:162-163]

✓ **Are the loyalties of the organization to God, His Messenger, and**
the believers at large?

إِنَّمَا وَلِيُّكُمُ ٱللَّهُ وَرَسُولُهُ وَٱلَّذِينَ ءَامَنُوا ٱلَّذِينَ يُقِيمُونَ ٱلصَّلَوٰةَ وَيُؤْتُونَ
ٱلزَّكَوٰةَ وَهُمْ رَٰكِعُونَ ۝ وَمَن يَتَوَلَّ ٱللَّهَ وَرَسُولَهُ وَٱلَّذِينَ ءَامَنُوا فَإِنَّ
حِزْبَ ٱللَّهِ هُمُ ٱلْغَٰلِبُونَ ۝

Your only guardians are Allah, His Messenger, and fellow
believers—who establish prayer and pay alms with humility.
Whoever allies themselves with Allah, His Messenger, and fellow
believers, then it is certainly Allah's party that will prevail. [5:55-56]

✓ *Is the organization's understanding and approach to Islam a*
balanced one?

The extremes of neglect and over-zealotry are to be avoided at all
costs, and nothing of Islam must be left out:

يَٰأَيُّهَا ٱلَّذِينَ ءَامَنُوا ٱدْخُلُوا فِى ٱلسِّلْمِ كَآفَّةً

O believers! Enter into Islam wholeheartedly... [2:208]

✓ *Does it develop the holistic Muslim personality, encour-*
aging every aspect of good character and citizenship, while
addressing flaws?

This is the group that will deserve the support and aid of Allah.
Allah says,

إِنَّ ٱللَّهَ لَا يُغَيِّرُ مَا بِقَوْمٍ حَتَّىٰ يُغَيِّرُوا مَا بِأَنفُسِهِمْ

Allah would never change a people's state until they change their
own state. [13:11]

قَدْ أَفْلَحَ مَن زَكَّىٰهَا ۝ وَقَدْ خَابَ مَن دَسَّىٰهَا ۝

Successful indeed is the one who purifies their soul, and doomed
is the one who corrupts it! [91:9-10]

✓ *Does the group aim to develop the Muslim personality on a community level and globally, even if indirectly?*

The scope of our Prophet's mission was universal:

$$وَمَآ أَرْسَلْنَٰكَ إِلَّا رَحْمَةً لِّلْعَٰلَمِينَ ۝$$

We have sent you only as a mercy for the whole world. [21:107]

✓ *Does the institution foster a network of individuals working for the same cause, uniting them upon common ideas and a shared mission?*

The Muslims share one heart and soul, no matter how numerous they are. This is why Allah instructs us to gather together for His cause:

$$وَٱعْتَصِمُوا بِحَبْلِ ٱللَّهِ جَمِيعًا وَلَا تَفَرَّقُوا$$

And hold firmly to the rope of Allah and do not be divided.
[3:103]

✓ *Does the organization operate with a nuanced awareness, grounded in knowledge and contemporary understanding?*

The organization's activity should be based on a deep understanding of the reality in which they operate. This is their responsibility and duty before Allah:

$$وَقُلِ ٱعْمَلُوا فَسَيَرَى ٱللَّهُ عَمَلَكُمْ وَرَسُولُهُ وَٱلْمُؤْمِنُونَ$$

Say "Do as you will. Your deeds will be seen by Allah, His Messenger, and the believers." [9:105]

Allah also says,

$$وَقُل لِّلَّذِينَ لَا يُؤْمِنُونَ ٱعْمَلُوا عَلَىٰ مَكَانَتِكُمْ إِنَّا عَٰمِلُونَ ۝$$

Say to those who disbelieve, "Persist in your ways; we will certainly persist in ours." [11:121]

✓ *Does the organization operate in light of priorities?*

Having priorities in order is vital to the legitimacy of any organization. When resources run scarce, an organization should be prepared to give precedence to foundational matters over secondary ones, and to address what is obligatory before branching out into what is supplementary. The Messenger of Allah ﷺ set this example when he undertook the mission of destroying the false gods within

106

the hearts of the people before destroying the physical idols to which they prayed.

✓ Does the group differentiate between foundational principles and secondary issues?

The former must be adhered to firmly, while secondary matters call for flexibility and pluralism. This accommodating approach allows for collaboration with all who share common, foundational goals, despite their minor differences.

✓ Does the group have clear and practical plans for growth?

The organizations we work with must have practical plans for growth and a scope that is clearly identified. They must be willing and able to help an individual grow steadily, outlining for them how to move from one stage to the next. Organizations must fulfill the ambitions of people in serving God, providing opportunities, addressing concerns, and empowering personal growth.

✓ Has the group proven itself capable of withstanding challenges?

Worthy organizations should be able to remain firm in the face of threats, political intimidation, and extremism. This is how leadership is earned, and this should be how we determine whom we follow. Allah guarantees us that this road comes with tests and challenges, and we must have exemplary models and support systems to prevail in those times:

$$وَلَنَبْلُوَنَّكُمْ حَتَّىٰ نَعْلَمَ الْمُجَاهِدِينَ مِنكُمْ وَالصَّابِرِينَ وَنَبْلُوَا۟ أَخْبَارَكُمْ ۝$$

We will certainly test you until We prove those of you who struggle and remain steadfast, and reveal how you conduct yourselves. [47:31]

✓ What is the organization's track record?

When possible, we should opt to work with organizations that are proven and established for longer periods of time. These are usually more established in their experience and knowledge of the path. The collective experience from which we can learn and build upon saves us time, energy and even money.

✓ *What are the organization's decision-making processes?*

The organization with which we work should be methodical and deliberate in its actions and decisions, for the reasons discussed under the chapter on hastening results. This is the mark of success for any successful individual or movement throughout history. Allah alludes to this when instructing the Prophet ﷺ to be patient in his mission:

$$\text{فَٱصْبِرْ كَمَا صَبَرَ أُو۟لُوا۟ ٱلْعَزْمِ مِنَ ٱلرُّسُلِ وَلَا تَسْتَعْجِل لَّهُمْ}$$

So endure patiently, as did the Messengers of Firm Resolve. And do not act in haste for them. [46:35]

✓ *Does the organization have wise and responsible leadership?*

The leadership of an organization is another important factor to consider when choosing with whom we should work. A director should be competent in doing exactly what their title states: guiding an institution in the right direction through proper structure and processes.

It is also important to see that the members of the organization comply with the directions they are given as long as they do not transgress Allah's boundaries. This does not mean that they cannot offer input; rather there should be an environment of mutual counsel, and decisions should be made through discussion. We should notice how these discussions are carried out, and whether empathy and courtesy are employed therein.

✓ *Does the organization hold itself and its membership of Islamic workers to high standards?*

This applies to the work the organization produces, as well as the quality of character among those who represent the organization and use it as a means of working for Islam.

✓ *Does the organization or group produce good results?*

It is imperative not only that our goals be in line with Allah and His Messenger ﷺ, but that we also take the means to achieve those goals. The golden standard for all of our work, individually or institutionally, must be that which the Prophet ﷺ and the early generations of righteous scholars after him set.

To justify improper means with virtuous ends is not appropriate. Anyone whose goal is to please Allah already has their route drawn out for them in the model of His Messenger ﷺ:

فَمَن كَانَ يَرْجُوا لِقَاءَ رَبِّهِ فَلْيَعْمَلْ عَمَلًا صَلِحًا

So whoever hopes for the meeting with their Lord, let them do good deeds... [18:110]

⁜ ⁜ ⁜ ⁜

ENDNOTES

1. al-Bukhari, v. 1, p. 11
2. Mulim, #1888
3. al-Bukhari, v. 9, p. 65; Muslim, #1847
4. Muslim, #1889
5. al-Tirmidhi, #2165
6. al-Tirmidhi, #2166
7. Ahmad, v. 4, p. 202
8. Abu Dawud, #4944
9. Abu Dawud, #4918
10. al-Bukhari, v. 3, p. 182
11. al-Tirmidhi, #2378
12. Abu Dawud, #4918
13. Ibn Qudāmah, Mukhtaṣar Minhāj al-Qāṣideen, p. 171
14. al-Bukhari, al-Adab al-Mufrad, #238
15. Ahmad, v. 6, p. 70
16. al-Tirmidhi, #2165
17. al-Bukhari, v. 3, p. 182
18. Muslim, #1848
19. Ibid., #2166
20. al-Bukhari, v. 9, p. 71
21. Ahmad, v. 4, p. 202

Self-Admiration

It's so easy for us as activists to fall into the trap of admiring ourselves and admiring the work we do. At first glance, I work harder, organize better, stay up later, and sacrifice more than most other people in my community. Even though my intentions started out good and sincere, it's so easy to fall into a false mindset, sitting back and thinking, "Wow, I did that."

Especially in a culture where a lot of us struggle with low self-esteem, we might cling to our actions and accomplishments to give us a sense of confidence. But that's not where our confidence should stem from—our confidence should be rooted in what is much more powerful than our fragile self. As soon as my sight fixes on my own self, accomplishments, legacy, and stature, I've actually become lost.

One of the roadblocks that many Muslim activists encounter and struggle with is self-admiration. Self-admiration is an early, reversible form of self-delusion and arrogance (addressed in the next two chapters). It is incumbent upon the Islamic worker to strive constantly to rid any traces of self-admiration and avoid it at all costs. In this chapter, we examine this roadblock carefully so as to better understand and prevent it.

Linguistically, the Arabic word *i'jāb* means to delight or impress. It appears often throughout the Quran. In the context of marriage, Allah clarifies that what looks pleasant at first glance (using the verb form of *i'jāb*) is not always better:

وَلَأَمَةٌ مُؤْمِنَةٌ خَيْرٌ مِّن مُّشْرِكَةٍ وَلَوْ أَعْجَبَتْكُمْ

*... a believing slave-woman is better than a free polytheist, even
though she may look pleasant to you. [2:221]*

Allah also points out that sometimes we are impressed by matters
that are filthy at their core:

قُل لَّا يَسْتَوِى ٱلْخَبِيثُ وَٱلطَّيِّبُ وَلَوْ أَعْجَبَكَ كَثْرَةُ ٱلْخَبِيثِ

*Say, "Purity and filth are not equal, though you may be dazzled by
the abundance of filth." [5:100]*

Allah compares those who are deluded by the transient glamour of
this world to farmers whose crops come to fruition, only to perish
soon after:

كَمَثَلِ غَيْثٍ أَعْجَبَ ٱلْكُفَّارَ نَبَاتُهُ ثُمَّ يَهِيجُ فَتَرَىٰهُ مُصْفَرًّا

*This is like rain that causes plants to grow, to the delight of the
planters. But later the plants dry up and you see them wither...*
[57:20]

The word *i'jāb* also refers to assuming mistakenly that something
is great and beneficial. Allah uses it in this way when he describes
the Muslim army's mistake of relying on their large numbers in the
Battle of Hunayn:

وَيَوْمَ حُنَيْنٍ إِذْ أَعْجَبَتْكُمْ كَثْرَتُكُمْ فَلَمْ تُغْنِ عَنكُمْ شَيْئًا

*... even at the Battle of Hunain when you took pride in your great
numbers, but they proved of no advantage to you. [9:25]*

When we use this word in the context of our role as Islamic
workers, teachers and activists, it takes on a more specific meaning.
I'jāb refers to being impressed by our own words or actions, regardless of their value in Allah's sight. Self-admiration is an early form of
the disease of arrogance—it is still free of transgression and underestimating others in the beginning. When this undue admiration for
the self is accompanied by a skewed perception of one's ability and
the merits of others, then it has evolved into self-delusion, which is
discussed in a later chapter. Self-delusion intensifies into what we

know as arrogance: extreme belittling of others and considering ourselves to be better than them in every way, leading to attitudes and actions that transgress and hurt others. Realizing that self-admiration is the first step in a cascading descent into arrogance should motivate us to extinguish it whenever its flames appear.

Causes of Self-Admiration

There are many reasons why this disease may develop in those who spend their time working for Islam. These causes include:

- Upbringing
- Un-Islamic praise
- Having conceited friends
- Ignoring the source of blessings
- Premature leadership
- Ignorance of the soul's nature
- Pride in heritage
- Excessive popularity
- Blind following
- Unawareness

UPBRINGING

How we are raised can affect how prone we are to self-admiration. We may have grown up in an environment where we learned to pursue praise and achievement (whether for positive or negative reasons) and to disregard the advice and criticism of others. This may be why Islam stresses that parents embed Islamic values into the household, because those values determine children's future tendencies. This concept of the home environment was discussed at length in earlier chapters. Allah's way of life guides parents to do well in the upbringing of their children, despite their inevitable human mistakes. Parents must employ Islamic values to the best of their ability and lead by example to show their children the practical application of Islam.

UN-ISLAMIC PRAISE

Islam provides guidelines for giving and receiving praise; when those guidelines are not observed, problems occur. Those who receive excessive praise beyond Islamic guidelines may develop narcissistic feelings. There are some people who will misinterpret praise to mean they are inherently exceptional, especially when that praise lacks the proper Islamic restrictions. The devil is always looking for an opening like this. This delusional idea settles in the mind and grows with every additional compliment thereafter, until an individual develops self-admiration or one of the more serious disease forms of self-delusion and arrogance—may Allah protect us all.

This is likely why the Prophet ﷺ discouraged praising people to their faces and taught us how, when it is necessary, to praise in a way that does not damage the soul and take advantage of its vulnerabilities. These guidelines that are provided throughout the Quran and Sunnah can be summarized into three main points: don't exaggerate, praise what is truly virtuous, and avoid praising those who are prone to vanity. Praise can be positive when it is intended to spur positive action, encourage someone to keep going, develop the habit of doing good, or identify someone as a good example for others to follow.

A man once stood up to praise a local government official in the presence of the Companion al-Miqdad bin al-Aswad. Al-Miqdad suddenly got up and began to throw dust in the face of the man, explaining, "The Messenger of Allah ﷺ instructed us to throw dust in the face of those who praise others excessively."[1] Another companion, Abu Bakrah, narrates that a man once praised another man in the presence of the Prophet ﷺ, and the Prophet ﷺ said, *"Beware, you've cut your fellow's throat! You've cut your fellow's throat!"* repeating it. He then said, *"Whenever one of you must praise his companion, he should say (so long as he knows the praise to be true), 'I consider him to be thus, and Allah is his judge—and I do not testify to the purity of anyone before Allah."*[2]

HAVING SELF-CENTERED FRIENDS

Spending time with people who admire and speak excessively about themselves can lead one to develop the same qualities. We naturally take on the habits and characteristics of our friends, especially those with very strong personalities. A person's conceit and self-admiration can sometimes be mistaken for confidence and success, and so his friends might emulate those traits in pursuit of the same aura. Islam instructs us to be selective in choosing the right companions to prevent the spread of this disease; we must spend our time with those who are humble, sincere and looking to grow.

IGNORING THE SOURCE OF BLESSINGS

Focusing on our gifts and blessings while neglecting the fact that they came from Allah can cause self-admiration and vanity. There are some Islamic workers who get caught up in the wealth, knowledge, or rank that Allah blessed them with while forgetting to remember where those blessings came from. They think, act, and even sometimes explicitly claim that they earned the blessing through virtue of their own efforts and capabilities, just as Qāroon did when he said,

إِنَّمَآ أُوتِيتُهُ عَلَىٰ عِلْمٍ عِندِىٓ

"I have been granted all this because of some knowledge I have." [28:78]

A person will keep repeating this until they believe they have achieved perfection, attributing all success and blessings to themselves.

This is the secret behind Islam's constant reminder of the source of our blessings. Allah says,

وَمَا بِكُم مِّن نِّعْمَةٍ فَمِنَ ٱللَّهِ

Whatever blessings you have are from Allah. [16:53]

Allah reminds us of our humble origins and how He endowed us with the basic senses with which we learn and navigate the world around us:

وَٱللَّهُ أَخْرَجَكُم مِّنۢ بُطُونِ أُمَّهَٰتِكُمْ لَا تَعْلَمُونَ شَيْـًٔا وَجَعَلَ لَكُمُ ٱلسَّمْعَ وَٱلْأَبْصَٰرَ وَٱلْأَفْـِٔدَةَ لَعَلَّكُمْ تَشْكُرُونَ ﴿﴾

And Allah brought you out of the wombs of your mothers while you knew nothing, and gave you hearing, sight, and intellect so perhaps you would be thankful. [16:78]

Allah created all that is around us for our own use and benefit, and teaches us to be thankful even for the blessings that we cannot detect:

$$\text{أَلَمْ تَرَوْا أَنَّ ٱللَّهَ سَخَّرَ لَكُم مَّا فِى ٱلسَّمَـٰوَٰتِ وَمَا فِى ٱلْأَرْضِ وَأَسْبَغَ عَلَيْكُمْ نِعَمَهُ ظَـٰهِرَةً وَبَاطِنَةً}$$

Have you not seen that Allah has subjected for you whatever is in the heavens and whatever is on the earth, and has lavished His favours upon you, both seen and unseen? [31:20]

And He challenges us to find someone else to sustain us if we reject Him as our Ultimate Provider:

$$\text{يَـٰٓأَيُّهَا ٱلنَّاسُ ٱذْكُرُوا نِعْمَتَ ٱللَّهِ عَلَيْكُمْ هَلْ مِنْ خَـٰلِقٍ غَيْرُ ٱللَّهِ يَرْزُقُكُم مِّنَ ٱلسَّمَآءِ وَٱلْأَرْضِ}$$

O humanity! Remember Allah's favours upon you. Is there any creator other than Allah who provides for you from the heavens and the earth? [35:3]

Additionally, the Prophet ﷺ taught us to say each morning and evening:

> Allah, not a single blessing has reached me or any of your creation except that it is from you—alone, without any partners—and so to you belongs all praise and to you belongs all gratitude.[3]

PREMATURE LEADERSHIP

Someone may develop self-admiration by taking on leadership roles in Islamic work before they're prepared for them. The conditions of Islamic work today often call for people to undertake tasks that they are not ready or qualified for. They take on heavy burdens before their shoulders are properly developed to carry them. This provides Satan with an opportunity to sneak in and convince them that they have such positions or responsibilities because they deserve it, and they will believe him if they are not careful. They begin to see themselves as more important or qualified than they actually are; this is the essence of *i'jāb* (self-admiration).

Thus, Islam teaches us to constantly search for more knowledge, deeper understanding, self-awareness and ways to improve ourselves all around. Allah draws our attention to the importance of properly learning before undertaking any responsibility. He says,

$$فَلَوْلَا نَفَرَ مِن كُلِّ فِرْقَةٍ مِّنْهُمْ طَآئِفَةٌ لِّيَتَفَقَّهُوا فِى ٱلدِّينِ وَلِيُنذِرُوا قَوْمَهُمْ إِذَا رَجَعُوٓا إِلَيْهِمْ لَعَلَّهُمْ يَحْذَرُونَ ۝$$

Only a party from each group should march forth, leaving the rest to gain religious knowledge then enlighten their people when they return to them, so that they may beware. [9:122]

Allah says, highlighting the virtue of wisdom, which is based on knowledge,

$$يُؤْتِى ٱلْحِكْمَةَ مَن يَشَآءُ وَمَن يُؤْتَ ٱلْحِكْمَةَ فَقَدْ أُوتِىَ خَيْرًا كَثِيرًا ۝$$

Allah grants wisdom to whoever He wills. And whoever is granted wisdom is certainly blessed with much good. [2:269]

The Prophet ﷺ echoed this when he said, *"Allah blesses anyone for whom He wishes well with understanding of the religion."*[4] Umar bin al-Khattab said, "Before you take on roles of leadership, learn."[5]

IGNORANCE OF THE SOUL'S NATURE

A lack of self awareness and being oblivious to the reality of our own egos can contribute to developing a sense of self-admiration. We often fail to remember that we all came from a sticky fluid that emerged from one organ into another. Ever since then our existence has been characterized by imperfection, and we are all heading towards the inevitable end of being buried in a hole in the ground where our bodies will decompose. When you forget this fact of your existence, it is easy to assume that you are exceptional, and Satan feeds into this notion until your self-admiration deteriorates into delusion and arrogance.

Allah and His Messenger address this reality over and over so that anyone who spends time reading the Quran and learning the teachings of our beloved Prophet ﷺ would not forget this humbling fact. Allah says,

الَّذِىٓ أَحْسَنَ كُلَّ شَىْءٍ خَلَقَهُۥ وَبَدَأَ خَلْقَ ٱلْإِنسَـٰنِ مِن طِينٍ ۝ ثُمَّ جَعَلَ
نَسْلَهُۥ مِن سُلَـٰلَةٍ مِّن مَّآءٍ مَّهِينٍ ۝

*Who has perfected everything He created. And He originated the
creation of humankind from clay. Then He made his descendants
from an extract of a humble fluid.* [32:7-8]

He reminds us where we came from and where we are headed:

أَلَمْ نَخْلُقكُّم مِّن مَّآءٍ مَّهِينٍ ۝

Did We not create you from a humble fluid [77:20]

ثُمَّ أَمَاتَهُۥ فَأَقْبَرَهُۥ ۝

He then causes them to die and be buried. [80:21]

PRIDE IN HERITAGE AND ETHNICITY

Pride in one's ethnicity or lineage can cause many of those involved
in Islamic activism to fall into self-admiration. This is because
many of those who are active come from families who have been
involved in dawah and Islamic work, with relatives who are well-
known leaders and scholars. This pride in heritage may even
manifest within immigrant communities that look down upon
indigenous and convert populations, or vice versa. Someone can
easily begin to think highly of themselves, neglecting that one's
ancestry can neither advance them nor hold them back in the sight
of Allah. All that He takes into consideration is our deeds and our
efforts, which can either extend a legacy of nobility or destroy it.

By placing value only in the individual's actions, Islam extin-
guishes the flames of ancestral pride. This is how Allah refined the
mindsets of Quraysh and the other Arab tribes—their pre-Islamic
culture was embedded with discrimination against others based
on tribal and ancestral lines. Repeated all throughout the scripture is the emphasis on valuing the true foundations of nobility
(righteousness and piety) rather than arbitrary social standards.
Allah says,

فَإِذَا نُفِخَ فِى ٱلصُّورِ فَلَآ أَنسَابَ بَيْنَهُمْ يَوْمَئِذٍ وَلَا يَتَسَآءَلُونَ ۝

Then, when the Trumpet will be blown, there will be no kinship
between them on that Day, nor will they ask about one another.
[23:101]

Allah's laws abolished any sense of inherent superiority. Virtue is only to be earned through action:

لَّيْسَ بِأَمَانِيِّكُمْ وَلَآ أَمَانِيِّ أَهْلِ ٱلْكِتَٰبِ مَن يَعْمَلْ سُوٓءًا يُجْزَ بِهِۦ وَلَا يَجِدْ
لَهُۥ مِن دُونِ ٱللَّهِ وَلِيًّا وَلَا نَصِيرًا ۝ وَمَن يَعْمَلْ مِنَ ٱلصَّٰلِحَٰتِ مِن ذَكَرٍ
أَوْ أُنثَىٰ وَهُوَ مُؤْمِنٌ فَأُو۟لَٰٓئِكَ يَدْخُلُونَ ٱلْجَنَّةَ وَلَا يُظْلَمُونَ نَقِيرًا ۝

It is neither by your wishes nor those of the People of the Book!
Whoever commits evil will be rewarded accordingly, and they will
find no protector or helper besides Allah. But those who do good—
whether male or female—and have faith will enter Paradise and will
never be wronged by as much as a speck on a date stone. [4:123-124]

When Allah sent down the verse,

وَأَنذِرْ عَشِيرَتَكَ ٱلْأَقْرَبِينَ ۝

And warn your closest relatives [26:214]

The Prophet ﷺ said to the tribe of Quraish,

> Purchase your souls from Allah! I can do nothing for you
> against Allah. Tribe of Abdul-Muttalib—I can do nothing
> for you against Allah. Abbas bin Abdul-Muttalib—I can do
> nothing for you against Allah. Safiyyah, aunt of Allah's Mes-
> senger—I can do nothing for you against Allah. Fatimah,
> daughter of Allah's Messenger—ask me for what you will,
> but I can do nothing for you against Allah.[6]

EXCESSIVE POPULARITY

Some personalities in the realm of Islamic work might gain a sense of popularity that exceeds the boundaries of what Islam dictates as appropriate (this is especially true in the social media culture in which numbers of followers is proof of neither truth, piety, wisdom or substance). A large following and their entailing admiration can

119

easily lead someone to become self-deluded and arrogant. The measures and expressions of popularity change from one culture and context to the next. Regardless of what this social popularity actually looks like, it can lead to a toxic admiration of the self, feeding into the presumption Satan plants in our minds that we deserve recognition for our efforts and capabilities. This notion grows stronger and its effect intensifies as the waves of compliments and displays of respect increase.

The Prophet ﷺ taught us to prevent this by setting guidelines for how his Companions interacted with him. For example, he prohibited them from standing up for him and from honoring him the way other cultures honored their kings. He sternly warned, *"Whoever loves that others stand for him should prepare his seat in the Hellfire."*[7] He once walked towards his Companions, leaning on a staff. When they stood up for him, he said, *"Do not stand like the non-Arabs stand for each other."*[8]

BLIND FOLLOWING

Some who engage in Islamic work will find that their personalities are charismatic and commanding. Those around them willingly adopt them as role models and follow their lead, regardless of the consequences or whether such authority is merited. Such blind compliance, wherein someone will follow and admire regardless of Allah's approval of the action, is not in line with Allah's teachings. Blind following of those around him can cause a leader to assume that they actually possess distinguished virtues and skills that others don't. This superiority complex is dangerous to one's faith and can lead to arrogance.

Islam does promote compliance with commands of those in charge, but only when the order does not involve any evil or sin. This compliance should be balanced with sound leadership, a process for giving advice, and *shura* (consultation). The story in the Quran of Prophet Sulaiman and the hoopoe bird is just one example of the values of compliance and consultation in action. The Prophet ﷺ said, *"Incumbent upon the Muslim person is to hear and obey what he may like or dislike, unless he is commanded to sin. If he is commanded to sin, then there is no obeying upon command."*[9]

LACK OF AWARENESS

As with all of the roadblocks discussed so far, a lack of awareness of oneself and the potential pitfalls lying in wait is one of the primary reasons for falling into spiritual disease. We make decisions based on our comprehension of the consequences that follow them. If someone is unaware of the harms of self-admiration and the dangers that it can lead to, they are at risk of falling into it unwittingly. They might underestimate it, not considering it as anything worthy of attention or correction. This ignorance may also manifest as a lack of awareness of the workings of our own mind and heart, not noticing subtle symptoms of disease. Thus, our religion urges us to understand this disease thoroughly, internalizing the gravity of its dangers, as well as monitoring our own behavior and thoughts.

Effects of Self-Admiration

Self-admiration has many harmful consequences that impair both the individual and the work that they do. Some of the effects on the individual include:

- Falling into greater diseases
- Being deprived of Allah's help
- Failing in times of difficulty
- Causing others to avoid us
- Facing Allah's punishment

FALLING INTO GREATER DISEASES

Self-admiration can intensify and deteriorate into delusion about oneself, and as a result, arrogance. Someone who is impressed with himself often tends to be inattentive to the state of his soul, neglecting to examine and hold himself accountable for his flaws. This only worsens over time, eventually leading to belittlement of others and feeling superior to them in all regards. Both self-delusion and arrogance come with a new set of dangers and harmful effects, which will be discussed in subsequent chapters.

BEING DEPRIVED OF ALLAH'S HELP

Those who are vain will often credit themselves with their own achievements. They rely on their own capabilities, forgetting that Allah is the One who created them, provided for them, and arranged all their affairs for them. He blessed them with all that they have, in addition to the countless blessings that go unnoticed.

This is nothing short of self-deception, and it leads to being deprived of Allah's divine assistance in anything they do. Of the many patterns observe in how Allah created the world around us is that he does not grant success to anyone unless they break free of their own ego and submit themselves wholly to Him. The successful are those who devote their lives to His worship and service. Allah says,

$$وَٱلَّذِينَ جَٰهَدُوا فِينَا لَنَهْدِيَنَّهُمْ سُبُلَنَا$$

As for those who struggle in Our cause, We will surely guide them to our paths. [28:69]

The Prophet ﷺ said that in a *hadith qudsi* that Allah said,

> My servant continues to come closer to me with voluntary actions until I love him. Then, when I love him, I am the hearing with which he hears, the vision with which he sees, the hand with which he strikes, and the foot with which he walks. If He asks of me, I will certainly give him, and if he seeks refuge in me, I will grant it to him.[10]

In order to secure such help from Allah, we must not delude ourselves into thinking that we are the originating source of any talent, blessing, achievement, or benefit.

FAILING IN TIMES OF DIFFICULTY

Those who think very highly of themselves will neglect to exert effort in self-purification. Their self-admiration convinces them that there is no need for any improvement, and they become complacent with their current state of character and spirituality. This is a recipe for failure, setting themselves up to burn out in the time of trial and hardship. They fail to develop a relationship with Allah in times of ease, and so when difficulty strikes, they find themselves alone. This is why Allah says,

$$إِنَّ ٱللَّهَ مَعَ ٱلَّذِينَ ٱتَّقَوا وَّٱلَّذِينَ هُم مُّحْسِنُونَ ۝$$

Surely Allah is with those who shun evil and who do good. [16:128]

$$وَإِنَّ ٱللَّهَ لَمَعَ ٱلْمُحْسِنِينَ ۝$$

And Allah is certainly with the good-doers. [29:69]

The Prophet ﷺ once said to his young cousin Abdullah bin Abbas, *"Stay mindful of Allah, and you will find Him in front of you. Make an effort to recognize Allah in times of ease, and He will recognize you in times of difficulty."*[11]

CAUSING PEOPLE TO AVOID US

Self-admiration and vanity earns us Allah's anger. This then brings about animosity from the people, as whomever Allah despises, the angels despise, and subsequently the people on earth feel inclined to despise them as well. People are naturally repulsed by those who are enamored with their own selves and tend to avoid their company. The Prophet ﷺ taught us this valuable lesson when he said,

> When Allah loves a servant, He calls Gabriel and says, "I love this person, so love him too." Gabriel then loves him, and so he calls out in the sky: "Allah loves this person, so love him too!" and then the inhabitants of the sky love him. Then affinity for him is placed on earth. When Allah despises a servant, He calls Gabriel and says, "I hate this person, so hate him too." Gabriel then hates him, and so he calls out to the inhabitants of the sky, "Allah hates this person, so hate him too." They then hate him, and so hatred for him is placed on earth.[12]

FACING ALLAH'S PUNISHMENT

Someone who is vain is bound to feel the effects of Allah's anger. It can occur immediately, such as when Allah caused the earth to swallow nations whole, or by something more subtle, such as damaged interpersonal relationships, loss of one's abilities, and so on. Allah can also choose to delay someone's punishment until they reach Hellfire, leading them further down the path of pain and heartbreak with every day they live. The Messenger of Allah ﷺ warned us about this when he recounted the story of a man from a previous nation: *"As a man was walking in a suit, impressed with himself and combing his hair, Allah seized him. Now he will plummet until the Day of Resurrection."*[13]

Community efforts and collective work are also harmed by the presence of self-admiration among Islamic workers. The Muslim community becomes increasingly vulnerable to corruption and attacks, and teamwork and effective group work becomes extremely difficult when individuals are afflicted with these diseases of the heart.

Those who are self-enamored will subject the projects and organizations in which they are involved to weakness and vulnerability. They hinder the workflow and impede effectiveness of the organization's efforts, raising costs and liabilities. Because of the high likelihood of those who are vain to fail under pressure, they put any organization with which they work at risk, in addition to the deprivation of any divine assistance or success.

Vain people are hard to get along with and rarely develop meaningful relationships. People generally don't like to associate themselves with those who are self-absorbed. This makes it difficult for an organization's team to accomplish anything substantial as it can ruin the chemistry and make for a toxic environment.

Symptoms of Self-Admiration

Self-admiration can be subtle and difficult to detect, but there are a few ways through which we can discover the degree to which we are affected by it. It is rare to find anyone who is completely free from the whisperings of self-admiration. One of the signs that self-admiration has infiltrated our soul is a tendency to praise ourselves. To constantly dwell on our own good deeds, pursuits, and virtues, overestimating our own value, means we may have forgotten that Allah knows the flaws and sins we keep hidden from the public. Allah says,

فَلَا تُزَكُّوٓا أَنفُسَكُمۡ هُوَ أَعۡلَمُ بِمَنِ ٱتَّقَىٰٓ ۝

So do not elevate yourselves. He knows best who is righteous. [53:32]

Another sign of encroaching self-admiration is that we become averse to receiving advice and criticism. Assuming perfection of oneself and rejecting the notion of improvement is indicative of one's vanity. Accepting the advice and suggestions of others is not only a sign of humility, but it is also a core component of developing a virtuous community.

A further indicator of vanity is that a person revels in hearing about the flaws and failures of others, especially their friends and peers. Such behavior is only born out of a desire to elevate the self. Al-Fudayl bin 'Iyād said, "One of the signs of a hypocrite is that they rejoice when they hear about the flaw of a peer."

Remedies for Self-Admiration

Now that we know the causes, effects, and symptoms of self-admiration, we can work hard to prevent it and cure it within ourselves. Its treatments include:

1. Remembering the nature of the ego
We must always remember that our souls came from the initial breath of life that Allah blew into us. Without it, we would not even exist. Our physical component is composed of the ground we walk on, and will end up being absorbed back into the soil as our corpses rot away deep under the ground. Your beautiful face will be consumed by maggots, and your sharp intellect will be of no help to you then. The living will cringe from the scent of your dead body, scrubbing the odor from their hands and cleansing it from their clothing. Remembering this often will keep us humble and recalibrate us when we stray, purging the traces of self-admiration and preventing us from falling further into it.

This is how the early generation of Muslims kept themselves in check. A wise man was once approached by someone who was quite impressed with himself, exclaiming pompously, "Do you know who I am?!" The wise man wittily responded, "Yes, I know who you are. You were once a filthy drop of fluid, and you will someday be a filthy corpse. And all the while—since your days as a fluid and until your days as a corpse—you are nothing more than a container for filth."

2. Remembering the reality of this world and the next

We must always understand the purpose of this present life; it is a planting ground for the seeds of the next life. And we must know that no matter how long it might last, it will ultimately come to an end. The afterlife is the only thing guaranteed to us, and the only life that is eternal. Keeping these realities in mind helps us maintain a balanced outlook and focused vision, encouraging us to put our affairs in order sooner rather than later.

3. Remembering Allah's blessings

By keeping in mind the countless blessings that Allah has showered upon us, which consume our existence from start to finish, we can always attribute any good we might see in ourselves to its true source: our Creator and Sustainer. Allah points out to us,

$$وَإِن تَعُدُّوا نِعْمَتَ ٱللَّهِ لَا تُحْصُوهَآ$$

If you tried to count Allah's blessings, you would never be able to number them. [14:34]

And He said,

$$وَأَسْبَغَ عَلَيْكُمْ نِعَمَهُ ظَاهِرَةً وَبَاطِنَةً$$

... and he has lavished His favours upon you, both seen and unseen... [31:20]

Remembering Allah as the source of all good helps us realize our own weakness and dependence on Him. We are constantly in need of Him, and anything we may find worthy of appreciation in ourselves is due entirely to Him.

4. Remembering death

Reflecting on death and what follows it keeps our hearts attentive and our insight sharp. The thought of death is a potent antidote to self-admiration. Imagining the moment that our souls depart this world and the stages of terror that follow is guaranteed to cleanse us of any vanity that might linger in our hearts, and redirect our focus from our own selves to matters more important.

5. A close relationship with the Quran and the Sunnah
Frequently reading and listening to the Quran, in addition to learning about the life and practice of the Prophet ﷺ, will keep us safe from the disease of self-admiration. The lessons and morals of humility and self-purification are patently clear therein. They offer a dynamic treatment for self-admiration through all of the aforementioned means of treatment, and are useful for helping anyone who is sincere in ridding themselves of any spiritual disease.

6. Frequently attending gatherings of learning
Spending time in environments centered around education and growth helps us pursue better versions of ourselves. This is especially true in the Muslim context, where topics and programming directly address the purification and refinement of the soul. Purification is the ultimate goal for learning any of the Islamic sciences. Attending these gatherings of knowledge helps us to prevent disease and recognize our own fallibility and need for improvement.

7. Visiting the sick
It is only a matter of time before our strength and beauty wither away. We can soften our hearts and break our self-admiration by exposing ourselves to the conditions of the ill and disabled, and to those who have recently died by washing their corpses, taking part in their funeral processions, and supplicating for them. Visiting the graveyard from time to time and reflecting on what the souls are experiencing also helps us keep this notion of fragility and temporality in mind.

8. Educating parents
Encouraging parents in our communities to be conscious of their parenting methods is an effective means of improving the conditions of our future generations. Drawing their attention to the harms of excessive praise in the raising of children, and to the importance of providing their children with an exemplary model of behavior in the

home can interrupt the cycle of negative impulses that perpetuate the diseases of pride and self-admiration in our communities. Parents can learn, repent and change their habits, and children learn a valuable lesson from witnessing this adjustment.

9. Avoiding those who are self-obsessed

Cutting out anyone in our lives who tends to be impressed with themselves and spending more of our time with the humble and unpretentious can help us become realistic and grounded. Being with such company and avoiding the opposite eases our transition out of this toxic behavior and prevents us from falling into it again.

10. Following the guidelines for praise

Complying with the Islamic guidelines for praising others can prevent us from promoting and spreading the disease of self-admiration and arrogance. Allah provided us with clear boundaries for showing respect and obeying our superiors. Transgressing those guidelines can result in stoking someone's admiration for themselves or intensifying the disease into one of its more destructive forms. Staying within the boundaries helps us keep one another from becoming incapacitated by roadblocks and falling prey to disease.

11. Avoiding unnecessary leadership

It might be necessary for some to refuse a position of leadership until they are sure that they are qualified and ready for it. In the meantime, they must refine their souls and work towards instilling humility so deeply in their core that a leadership position would not corrupt them. This humility will be their armor and ammunition against Satan, who works tirelessly to plant seeds of self-admiration into the hearts of anyone with any rank of leadership.

12. Learning about the lives of the early Muslims

Exposing ourselves to the virtue and humility of the early generation of Companions and scholars is a solid strategy in preventing any delusion about our own righteousness and merit. Despite the high level of character and achievement they attained, they were still not enamored with their own selves or infatuated with their accomplishments. We can marvel at how they used to react when they would be praised or sensed traces of self-admiration within themselves. This knowledge will help us follow their example and emulate them, following their formulas of acting and speaking.

13. Breaking the ego

From time to time, it is a good idea to subject ourselves to circumstances that break our sense of vanity, putting us in our proper places and reminding us of our true nature. We can volunteer for acts of service in our communities that aren't so glorious and esteemed, making sure to avoid sharing with the world our reasons for doing so. This includes spending time with those who are less fortunate, running errands for our elderly relatives and community members, and performing acts of physical labor for others, such as preparing meals, doing household chores, repairing a car, and so on.

This was a method that many of the early Muslims took advantage of. Umar bin al-Khattab, for example, encountered a passage filled with water on his way to Syria. He dismounted his camel, took off his socks, and waded through the water with his bare feet, holding his camel by the reins. Abu Ubaydah noticed how Umar had diminished himself, and said to him, "You did something that others would deem preposterous!" Umar struck him on his chest and said, "If only it were anyone but you, Abu Ubaydah! You were the most disgraced and miserable of people, and then Allah honored you with His Messenger. If you ever seek honor through anything else, Allah will disgrace you."

In a similar story, it says that people came to Umar as he was approaching Syria and advised him to ride a horse instead of his homely camel, as he was about to meet with noble company. Umar responded, "I don't take you all here into consideration. The only one whose opinion I take into consideration is there," and he pointed upwards towards the sky. "Now leave my camel alone," he commanded.

14. Peer support

It is helpful in any endeavor to have support. In ridding ourselves of vanity, we can ask some of our close companions whose opinions we trust to keep an eye on our behavior. They can alert us to any actions or words that might indicate that we have fallen victim to this roadblock of self-admiration, coaching us on our road to improvement. In the company of other righteous people, we can access so many new resources in our quest of purification and self-awareness.

15. Holding ourselves accountable
Paying close attention to what we do and say, and assessing our intentions helps us to straighten out the kinks within us. Self-accountability helps us notice our flaws in real-time and gives us a chance to catch them before they grow into an unwieldy, diseased pattern of behavior.

16. Understanding the consequences
Internalizing the true degree of harm that comes with vanity and self-admiration strikes an urgent fear within us to rid ourselves of it. It is an effective way for us to purge ourselves of it and protect ourselves from falling further into it.

17. Asking Allah for help
Seeking help from Allah, Mighty and Majestic, in our prayers from internal diseases and roadblocks is the greatest key to defeating them. When we turn to Him, He turns towards us, and when we seek purity through Him, He purifies us. He is our sole Supporter and Sustainer.

18. Taking responsibility
We must understand that we are responsible for ourselves and our actions. Our social class, family ancestry and legacy is of no benefit to us with Allah. This realization helps us purify ourselves of vanity and come closer to Allah through sincere actions, rather than being deluded by our own merit and contribution.

✦ ✦ ✦

ENDNOTES

1. Muslim, #3002
2. al-Bukhari, v. 8, p. 22; and Muslim, #3000 (in this wording)
3. Abu Dawud, #5073
4. al-Bukhari, v. 4, p. 103; Muslim, #1037
5. al-Bukhari, v. 1, p. 28
6. al-Bukhari, v. 6, p. 140; Muslim, #206 (in this wording)
7. Abu Dawud, #5229
8. Abu Dawud, #5230
9. Muslim, #1839
10. al-Bukhari, v. 7, p. 131
11. Ahmad, v. 1, p. 307
12. al-Bukhari, v. 4, p. 135; Muslim, #2637 (in this wording)
13. al-Bukhari, v. 7, p. 183 (in this wording); Muslim, 2088

Self-Delusion

When self-admiration is not checked and addressed, it may develop into a new roadblock and disease—*al-ghuroor*, translated as self-delusion. Self-delusion is defined as a failure to recognize reality and an excessively favorable opinion of one's own abilities and importance, and this seems a suitable translation for the delusion of ghuroor. Self-admiration, delusion, and arrogance are interconnected; when one is not checked it will often exacerbate and take on a new form. We will attempt in this chapter to understand the nature of self-delusion and analyze it in order to defeat and prevent it.

> I've witnessed it time and again with severe consequences for our community—the community trusts a leader or a group of leaders with leading an institution. Time, efforts, and funds pour in, and Allah blesses our efforts and the institution flourishes and starts to have a positive impact. But when it is time for the founders to move on and hand the baton to the next generation, they resist and declare, "We are the ones who built the organization", "No one knows better", "We are the only ones who have the experience!"
>
> Preservation of leadership becomes their main goal because they had grown impressed by their own actions and dedication. Eventually, the community moves on, and the institution stagnates under a weak, unpopular leadership. This fatal malady of conceit and arrogance not only impacts individual activists but also continues to cost our community dearly on both the local, regional and national levels.

Ghuroor, the Arabic word for delusion, carries a number of meanings and connotations. Its root alludes to a sense of deception either toward or from others, or both simultaneously. Allah uses the word in the Quran in the following ayah,

$$وَمَا يَعِدُهُمُ ٱلشَّيْطَـٰنُ إِلَّا غُرُورًا ۝$$

Truly Satan promises them nothing but <u>delusion.</u> [4:120]

The word *ghuroor* can also refer not only to deception, but also anything that leads to deception. It may refer to the means and tools of delusion, whether wielded against the self or others. Allah uses it in this manner when He says,

$$يَـٰٓأَيُّهَا ٱلنَّاسُ إِنَّ وَعْدَ ٱللَّهِ حَقٌّ فَلَا تَغُرَّنَّكُمُ ٱلْحَيَوٰةُ ٱلدُّنْيَا وَلَا يَغُرَّنَّكُم بِٱللَّهِ$$
$$ٱلْغَرُورُ ۝$$

O humanity! Indeed, Allah's promise is true. So do not let the life of this world <u>deceive you</u>, nor let the <u>Chief Deceiver</u> <u>deceive</u> you about Allah. [35:5]

Since this book addresses roadblocks in the Islamic activist's journey, *ghuroor* in this context refers to an advanced, deluded stage of self-admiration wherein we start to belittle the actions and words of others, constantly comparing it to what we do or can do. It is a lesser form of arrogance that comes before belittling the actual person themselves or considering ourselves to be inherently superior—arrogance will be addressed in depth in the next chapter. *Ghuroor,* or delusion, is an apt term associated with this advanced stage of self-admiration because someone who believes their work to be better than anyone else's is suffering from a sort of deception.

An Easy Misconception

We might think that looking down on a project or approach is completely valid, since we are criticizing the work not the people. However, this is the exact attitude of *ghuroor,* in which we are belittling the deeds and efforts of others, and feeling good about ourselves in the process.

This is a dangerous form of self-delusion, since it is so much easier to sit on the sidelines and inflate one's ego than to actually join hands with others and do the work.

There are a number of signs that one might be suffering from the disease of self-delusion. The first is that they find themselves undermining and belittling the efforts of others, even when the effort is purely good. You will also find those who are deluded by their own self-image constantly mentioning their own work with praise. Those who are self-deluded are reluctant to accept advice when it is contrary to their inflated view of themselves. They find it extremely difficult to concede to the truth when it is presented to them, even by their teachers and more experienced members of their communities.

Causes of Self-Delusion

Self-delusion is an evolved form of self-admiration, so we can include among its causes those listed in the previous chapter. But there are also additional causes for delusion; catalysts that spark its growth from mere vanity to this more severe stage.

- Neglecting self-assessment
- Being neglected by others
- Excessiveness in religion
- Increasing knowledge without increasing effort
- Being oblivious to our sins
- Investing in this life
- Having bad role models
- Differential treatment
- Excessive secrecy in good deeds

NEGLECTING SELF-ASSESSMENT

Failing to hold ourselves accountable and assess ourselves can lead to self-delusion. Some of those who work for Islam might already have been afflicted with self-admiration, and due to lack of attention to their own flaws and missteps, the disease settles within them and grows. It develops from being merely impressed with one's own actions to belittling everyone else in comparison and seeing oneself as intrinsically superior—a sign of true self-delusion. This may be the secret behind Islam's emphatic encouragement of self-assessment and holding ourselves accountable for our actions. As Allah instructs us,

يَـٰٓأَيُّهَا ٱلَّذِينَ ءَامَنُوا۟ ٱتَّقُوا۟ ٱللَّهَ وَلْتَنظُرْ نَفْسٌ مَّا قَدَّمَتْ لِغَدٍ ۖ وَٱتَّقُوا۟ ٱللَّهَ ۚ إِنَّ
ٱللَّهَ خَبِيرٌۢ بِمَا تَعْمَلُونَ ۝

*O believers! Be mindful of Allah and let every soul look to what it
has sent forth for tomorrow. And fear Allah, certainly Allah is All-
Aware of what you do.* [59:18]

BEING NEGLECTED BY OTHERS

A deluded sense of self can also evolve when people fail to pay attention to us, or fail to care enough to help us defeat these diseases
when they see their signs within us. Some of us do not have enough
strength or motivation to undertake the task of self-purification
without assistance or mentorship. It might be within someone's personality that they depend on the support and guidance of others in
order to examine their own motivations. But if those around them
don't realize this, failing to fulfill their role and duty to their fellow
community members, then the disease will settle within them and
grow with time—God protect us all.

This may be the reason why Islam so wisely promotes a sincere
dedication to helping one another. It is a defining quality that the
Prophet ﷺ used to describe the religion when he said, *"Religion
is sincere allegiance."* His Companions asked, *"To whom?"* He
responded, *"To God, to His Scripture, to His Messenger, and to the
leaders of the Muslims and their populace."*[1] Allah also urges us to
work together, as He says,

وَتَعَاوَنُوا۟ عَلَى ٱلْبِرِّ وَٱلتَّقْوَىٰ

Cooperate with one another in goodness and righteousness... [5:2]

The Prophet ﷺ said,

> The believer is a mirror for his fellow believer, and a believer
> is a brother to his fellow believer. He prevents him from loss
> and protects him from behind.[2]

EXCESSIVENESS IN RELIGION

Being excessive and overzealous in our religious practice can certainly lead to self-delusion. Some who work for Islam approach God's

religion with excessive zeal, and after a while look around them and observe that others may not be practicing as strictly as they are. They then develop the deluded idea, out of ignorance of Islam's balance, that those who don't approach it as intensely as they do are falling short, and this assumption leads them to undermine the actions of their peers.

Islam calls us to moderation and warns against excessiveness and extremism. The Prophet 變 said, for example, to the group of young men who mistakenly assumed it was better to remain celibate and completely immersed in ritual worship:

> You have said this and that, but by Allah, I am the most fearful of Allah of you all, and the most cognizant of Him out of you. Yet I fast and I eat, I pray and I sleep, and I marry women. So whoever is averse to my way is not associated with me.[3]

The Prophet 變 also warned very sternly, *"Doomed are those who transgress to extremes!"*[4] repeating it three times over. In another hadith, he said, *"Beware of excessiveness in religion, for those before you only perished because of excessiveness in religion."*[5] He also said,

> The religion is ease, and no one goes to extremes in the religion except that it overwhelms him. So aim straight, come as close as you can, and rejoice.[6]

INCREASING KNOWLEDGE WITHOUT INCREASING EFFORT

Learning and attaining Islamic knowledge can lead to deluded self-importance, especially for those who focus on matters of contention or topics that are very technical while neglecting to increase their efforts to purify themselves. Some Islamic workers like to dive deep into technical issues of knowledge that others are not familiar with. The more they realize that most of the people are ignorant of what they know, the more they begin to think of their knowledge and actions as superior to others.

These individuals fail to realize that others may not know the information that they know because it is, in fact, non-essential to the actual implementation of the religion. They constantly compare their depth of knowledge on these particular topics to the lack of understanding by others, thereby belittling their knowledge of the religion altogether.

To prevent this Islam emphasizes the importance of focusing our learning only on that which is beneficial and useful. The Prophet ﷺ himself would pray,

> Allah, I take refuge with you from knowledge that does not benefit, from a heart that is not fearful, from a spirit that is insatiable, and from a supplication that is not answered.[7]

Allah also teaches us in the Quran the importance of accompanying our knowledge with action. He says,

$$يَـٰٓأَيُّهَا ٱلَّذِينَ ءَامَنُوا۟ لِمَ تَقُولُونَ مَا لَا تَفْعَلُونَ ۝ كَبُرَ مَقْتًا عِندَ ٱللَّهِ أَن تَقُولُوا۟ مَا لَا تَفْعَلُونَ ۝$$

O believers! Why do you say what you do not do? How despicable it is in the sight of Allah that you say what you do not do! [61:2-3]

Allah criticizes those who don't put into practice the values that they preach, connecting this cognitive dissonance to a lack of actual understanding:

$$أَتَأْمُرُونَ ٱلنَّاسَ بِٱلْبِرِّ وَتَنسَوْنَ أَنفُسَكُمْ وَأَنتُمْ تَتْلُونَ ٱلْكِتَـٰبَ ۚ أَفَلَا تَعْقِلُونَ ۝$$

Do you preach righteousness and fail to practice it yourselves, although you read the Scripture? Do you not understand? [2:44]

The Prophet ﷺ warned of a specific punishment in Hell for those whose actions don't match up with their teachings:

> A man will be brought forth on the Day of Resurrection and thrown into the fire. His intestines will pour forth, and he will roam around with them as a donkey roams around with a millstone. The people of the hellfire will gather to him and say: "So-and-so, what happened to you? You used to encourage good and condemn evil." He will say: "I would encourage good that I myself would not engage in. And I would condemn evil that I myself would engage in.[8]

BEING OBLIVIOUS TO OUR SINS

Another mistake that might lead someone to falling into self-delusion is that they are solely focused on their good deeds while ignoring their sins and flaws. We are all human beings, and all humans (except for the Prophets) are subject to error. Forgetting this reality will result in seeing only our good qualities and being oblivious to our mistakes, while simultaneously perceiving others through a flipped lens: seeing only their flaws and negative qualities and ignoring their strengths. This undoubtedly leads to a deluded, misguided belittlement of other's actions.

True believers are far removed from this toxic perception of oneself and others. Allah praises a certain group of believers who fulfill their duties, while still fearing that their efforts are flawed and insufficient:

إِنَّ ٱلَّذِينَ هُم مِّنْ خَشْيَةِ رَبِّهِم مُّشْفِقُونَ ۞ وَٱلَّذِينَ هُم بِـَٔايَـٰتِ رَبِّهِمْ يُؤْمِنُونَ ۞ وَٱلَّذِينَ هُم بِرَبِّهِمْ لَا يُشْرِكُونَ ۞ وَٱلَّذِينَ يُؤْتُونَ مَآ ءَاتَواْ وَّقُلُوبُهُمْ وَجِلَةٌ أَنَّهُمْ إِلَىٰ رَبِّهِمْ رَٰجِعُونَ ۞ أُوْلَـٰٓئِكَ يُسَـٰرِعُونَ فِى ٱلْخَيْرَٰتِ وَهُمْ لَهَا سَـٰبِقُونَ ۞

Surely those who tremble in awe of their Lord, and who believe in the revelations of their Lord, and who associate none with their Lord, and who do whatever they do with their hearts fearful that they will return to their Lord—it is they who race to do good deeds, always taking the lead. [23:57-61]

Aishah once asked the Prophet ﷺ about the implications of the verse quoted above, "[those] who do whatever they do with their hearts fearful that they will return to their Lord..." [23:60]. She asked, "Is this talking about the one who steals, fornicates, and drinks wine while he fears Allah, Mighty and Majestic?" The Prophet ﷺ said, "*No, daughter of al-Siddeeq; rather they are those who fast, pray, and give charity while fearing that it will not be accepted from them...*" (the hadith continues)[9]

The Prophet ﷺ also called our attention to the dangers of self-delusion when he emphasized the importance of attributing success to God's grace and mercy, rather than one's own efforts. He said, "*No one's deeds will save him.*" His Companions asked, "*Not even you,*

Messenger of Allah?" He responded,

> Not even me, unless Allah envelops me in His mercy. Aim straight, come close, and work throughout the morning, the evening, and for some of the night time. Moderation! With moderation you shall prevail.[10]

Abdullah bin Mas'ood also expressed this concept clearly. He made clear how important it is for us to remember our sins for the sake of our own spiritual refinement. He said,

> The believer is one who sees his own sins as if he is sitting beneath a mountain, fearing that it might fall over on him. The wicked person is one who sees his sins like a fly that passes over his nose, and so he just shoos it away.[11]

INVESTING IN THIS LIFE

Being too invested and enamoured with this life can be what drives someone to a sense of delusion. Some may detect the traces of self-admiration, but find themselves too lazy or unmotivated to counteract the disease, procrastinating in their repentance. Such a person is too attached to the payoffs and pleasures that come from a vain, conceited attitude. As time passes, the roots of self-admiration plunge deeper and evolve into delusion.

Allah calls our attention to the dangers of delusion often throughout the Quran. Much of the discourse in the Quran is dedicated to pointing out the worthlessness of this life and warning against making it our main priority. Allah says,

اعْلَمُوٓا أَنَّمَا ٱلْحَيَوٰةُ ٱلدُّنْيَا لَعِبٌ وَلَهْوٌ وَزِينَةٌ وَتَفَاخُرٌ بَيْنَكُمْ وَتَكَاثُرٌ فِى ٱلْأَمْوَٰلِ وَٱلْأَوْلَٰدِ كَمَثَلِ غَيْثٍ أَعْجَبَ ٱلْكُفَّارَ نَبَاتُهُۥ ثُمَّ يَهِيجُ فَتَرَىٰهُ مُصْفَرًّا ثُمَّ يَكُونُ حُطَٰمًا وَفِى ٱلْءَاخِرَةِ عَذَابٌ شَدِيدٌ وَمَغْفِرَةٌ مِّنَ ٱللَّهِ وَرِضْوَٰنٌ وَمَا ٱلْحَيَوٰةُ ٱلدُّنْيَآ إِلَّا مَتَٰعُ ٱلْغُرُورِ ﴿٢٠﴾

Know that this worldly life is no more than play, amusement,
luxury, mutual boasting, and competition in wealth and children.
This is like rain that causes plants to grow, to the delight of the
planters. But later the plants dry up and you see them wither, then
they are reduced to chaff. [57:20]

He also says,

وَٱضۡرِبۡ لَهُم مَّثَلَ ٱلۡحَيَوٰةِ ٱلدُّنۡيَا كَمَاءٍ أَنزَلۡنَٰهُ مِنَ ٱلسَّمَاءِ فَٱخۡتَلَطَ بِهِۦ نَبَاتُ ٱلۡأَرۡضِ فَأَصۡبَحَ هَشِيمًا تَذۡرُوهُ ٱلرِّيَٰحُ وَكَانَ ٱللَّهُ عَلَىٰ كُلِّ شَىۡءٍ مُّقۡتَدِرًا ۝

And give them a parable of this worldly life: like the plants of the earth, thriving when sustained by the rain We send down from the sky. Then they turn into chaff scattered by the wind. And Allah is fully capable of all things. [18:45]

And He says,

إِنَّ ٱلَّذِينَ لَا يَرۡجُونَ لِقَآءَنَا وَرَضُواْ بِٱلۡحَيَوٰةِ ٱلدُّنۡيَا وَٱطۡمَأَنُّواْ بِهَا وَٱلَّذِينَ هُمۡ عَنۡ ءَايَٰتِنَا غَٰفِلُونَ ۝ أُوْلَٰئِكَ مَأۡوَىٰهُمُ ٱلنَّارُ بِمَا كَانُواْ يَكۡسِبُونَ ۝

Indeed, those who do not expect to meet Us, being pleased and content with this worldly life, and who are heedless of Our signs, they will have the Fire as a home because of what they have committed. [10:7-8]

The Prophet ﷺ said,

> Doomed is the servant of the dinar, the servant of the dirham, and the servant of the garment, who is pleased when given and angered when he is not. May he perish forever, and when he is harmed, may he never recover! Congratulations to a servant who holds the reins of his horse in the path of Allah, with his disheveled hair and his dusty feet. When he is placed on the front lines, he stands on the front lines, and when he is placed at the back, he stands at the back. When he seeks permission, he is denied, and when he offers his input, it is declined.[12]

The Companions recount that the Prophet ﷺ would rarely ever end a gathering before he said the following words of prayer:

> O Allah, apportion for us enough fear of you that will prevent us from disobeying You; and enough of Your obedience that will deliver us to your Paradise; and enough certainty that will make the afflictions of this world easy for us. Grant us the enjoyment of our hearing, our vision, and our strength as long as we live, never being deprived of it. Avenge us against those who wronged us and support us against those who oppose us. Do not afflict us in our

religious commitment, do not make this life our primary concern nor the extent of our knowledge, and do not give those who will not show us mercy authority over us.[13]

The early generations of Muslims understood very well the worthlessness of this life. They would only engage in it to the extent that it benefitted their Afterlife, stating their intentions clearly to remind themselves and those around them of the true purpose of our time on earth. Ali bin Abu Talib said,

> This world is soon to depart, and the afterlife is soon to arrive, and each of them has their people. Be people of the afterlife, and do not be people of this life, for today is for actions, not judgments, and tomorrow is for judgments, not actions.[14]

Al-Hasan al-Basri once said, "Race against anyone who competes with you for the religion, but whoever competes with you for this life, let him have it."[15] There is an insightful poem that goes:

> *There are some servants of Allah who smartly invest*
> *They divorce this world fearing its tests*
> *When they saw it they knew*
> *That its tricks weren't true*
> *They treated it like an ocean,*
> *and their deeds were life vests.*

HAVING BAD ROLE MODELS

Someone may be driven to self-delusion after witnessing some of the role models or leaders in their communities behave in ways unbecoming of them. Some community leaders fail to uphold the values and standards that they should be promoting through leading by example. They often forego acts that are virtuous but voluntary, and fall into the gray area between permissible and prohibited.

This not only weakens the moral condition of the community at large, but leads those who hold themselves to higher standards of morality to begin to question the validity of leadership. Those who are already impressed by their own level of practice will see themselves as superior and more worthy of leadership than existing community leaders. Their self-admiration feeds off of the low quality of leadership and may then transform into delusion and belittlement of those same leaders.

In order to prevent this, Islam encourages us to avoid anything that might hinder our reputation as leaders. It is also important to clarify our own innocence when engaging in something that an uninformed observer might assume to be sinful. In a touching illustration of this, Safiyyah, the wife of the Prophet ﷺ, narrates that she once came to visit the Prophet ﷺ in the mosque as he was in his devotional retreat there during the last ten nights of Ramadan. She stayed there speaking to him for a while, and then got up to return home. The Prophet ﷺ got up to walk with her, and when they reached the door in the mosque that led to Umm Salamah's apartment, two men from the Ansar passed by and greeted the Messenger of Allah ﷺ. The Messenger of Allah ﷺ said to them, "Be easy, it is only Safiyyah bint Huyay." They exclaimed, "Subhān Allah, Messenger of Allah!" shocked that the Prophet ﷺ would feel the need to clarify his actions to them. But he said to them, *"Satan runs as deep in a human as blood, and I feared that he would cast something into your hearts."*[16]

Another Companion named Yazeed bin al-Aswad once prayed with the Prophet ﷺ while he was a young boy. He narrates that as the Prophet ﷺ was praying, there were two men sitting at the side of the mosque who were not praying. He called for them, and when they were brought over, their shoulders were trembling. The Prophet ﷺ asked, *"What prevented you from praying with us?"* They responded, "We had already prayed in our homes." He said, *"Do not do that. When any of you prays in his home, and then catches the Imam who has yet to pray, pray with him, for it will be a voluntary act for him."*[17] The instruction of the Prophet to these two men served to protect their reputation (since not praying with the congregation could have garnered the criticism of others) and also to elevate the unity and observance of the community as a whole.

Ibn Daqeeq al-'Eed said that taking steps to avoid the suspicions of others is even more important for scholars and leaders. He said, "It is not permissible for them to do anything that might cause others to think ill of them, even if they are completely innocent therein."[18] He said that it would prevent people from benefiting from their knowledge if there was even the slightest doubt of their moral integrity.

EXCESSIVE SECRECY IN GOOD DEEDS

We can also become deluded about our own righteousness by failing to realize that there are people among us who take advanced measures to hide their worship and good deeds. These devoted people outperform everyone around them and are highly motivated to preserve their sincerity, and so they take every step necessary to hide the good they do. They read Quran, pray extra prayers, visit the sick, give charity, serve the disadvantaged, all while the community is unaware of their doings. Those who have not yet developed such concealment in their own works might then assume the actions of these sincere workers to be insignificant. They would compare their deeds only to what is visible of others, and eventually develop a sense of superiority over their peers whose efforts are less public.

Perhaps Islam's invitation to publicize our good deeds in some cases so as to motivate others is related to the preventing individuals from becoming deluded about the quantity of their deeds. Allah says,

إِن تُبْدُواْ ٱلصَّدَقَٰتِ فَنِعِمَّا هِىَ ۖ وَإِن تُخْفُوهَا وَتُؤْتُوهَا ٱلْفُقَرَآءَ فَهُوَ خَيْرٌ لَّكُمْ ۚ وَيُكَفِّرُ عَنكُم مِّن سَيِّـَٔاتِكُمْ

To give charity publicly is good, but to give to the poor privately is better for you, and will absolve you of your sins. [2:271]

The Prophet ﷺ also alluded to the importance of public displays of good when he encouraged us to pray the communal prayers inside of the mosque: *"The communal prayer is twenty-seven times more superior to the individual prayer."*[19] He also taught us the importance of making good traditions and practices widespread by teaching them to others and leading by example:

> Whoever established a good practice in Islam has its reward and the reward of whoever does it after him, without taking away from any of their rewards at all.[20]

DIFFERENTIAL TREATMENT

When leaders treat some members, individuals, or volunteers differently than others, forgetting the importance of fair and equal treatment, this can promote the roadblock of self-delusion within the community. These individuals who are treated preferentially and with more respect might assume they are more worthy than others. Due to personal relationships, their mistakes and the flaws in their work may be excused more readily than others, allowing them to remain at their leadership positions while holding others are held to more stringent standards of accountability.

This nepotism and unequal treatment is how positions in institutions are easily filled with unqualified and immature people, whose lack of experience and professionalism manifests in their work. Such unqualified people can easily be led to believe they earned these positions due to skills and capabilities they assume others lack. Eventually, they will assume their work and their qualifications are greater than all those around them.

The Prophet ﷺ actively prevented this by treating all of the Companions fairly. They used to describe him by saying, *"He would give everyone who sat with him their due share. No one in his company ever thought that there was anyone more generous to them than him."*[21] If ever the Prophet ﷺ saw a need to differentiate between some of his Companions in how he treated them, he would clarify to those around him what his objective was.

Sa'd bin Abu Waqqās narrates that the Messenger of Allah ﷺ once gave some funds to a group of people, but he left off one man who was the most impressive among them. Sa'd asked, "Messenger of Allah, what about that man? By Allah, I see him to be a believer." He ﷺ said, "Rather, a Muslim." Sa'd stayed silent for a while, but then his assumptions overwhelmed him, so he repeated his question: "What about that man? By Allah, I see him to be a believer." He said again, "Rather, a Muslim." Again, his assumption overwhelmed him, and so he repeated his question, and the Messenger of Allah ﷺ repeated his response. Then the Messenger of Allah ﷺ said, *"Sa'd, I might give to one man while another is more beloved to me, out of fear that Allah might cast him into the Hellfire."*[22]

Effects of Self-Delusion

Self-delusion carries many harmful effects and dangerous consequences that affect the workers individually and the work that they do. Some

145

of its effects on the individual include being overly argumentative, dogmatic, and eventually growing arrogant.

ARGUMENTATIVE TENDENCIES

An individual afflicted with self-delusion will tend to have combative tendencies. He or she has an intense self-admiration and sees their actions as superior to everyone else's, and so they will always attempt to prove this to those around him. Satan convinces them that the best way to do this is to debate everything and demonstrate their superiority. So they proceed to waste much time senselessly arguing.

The Prophet ﷺ taught us the dangers of arguing too much. He said, *"A nation has never gone astray after having been upon guidance except that they were given argumentation."*[23] He ﷺ also highlighted how dangerous being quarrelsome and engaging in too much debate can be when he promised a lofty reward for those who avoid it:

> I guarantee a house in the outskirts of Paradise for anyone who leaves off arguing, even if he is right; and a house in the center of Paradise for anyone who leaves off lying, even when he is joking, and a house at the peak of Paradise for whoever's character is beautiful.[24]

FALLING INTO ARROGANCE

Another individual effect of self-delusion is falling into arrogance. After the trait of self-admiration builds up into delusion, it continues to deteriorate from belittling what others say and do to belittling the people themselves and feeling superior to them. Arrogance will be discussed further in the last chapter.

DOGMATISM

Self-delusion can also lead to being dogmatic in our opinions. Someone who thinks highly of their own opinions and believes everything they do and think is superior, while assuming by default that everyone else is wrong, will not concede to the truth if it contradicts the opinion they hold. They will continue to be wrong and make mistakes until they die or disgrace themselves beyond repair.

When volunteers and Islamic workers are afflicted with a deluded sense of self, it has a terrible impact on community work and service. It makes their efforts fragile and vulnerable to the enemies of Allah. It also reduces the effectiveness of their work, their reputation, and that of any organization they work with. For any work that they do, people will only see the conceited personalities behind it, and will be repelled by that aura of vanity and self-importance. The public image and support for those individuals and the institutions they serve will suffer, especially during times of difficulty.

Cures for Self-Delusion

It is very possible to rid ourselves of self-delusion once we are thoroughly aware of its presence and recognize its symptoms and causes. We should learn how to trace the development of disease from self-admiration to delusion to arrogance, recognizing the symptoms of each stage. More importantly, we must know how to prevent this disease from overtaking us or worsening into a more serious form. The following are treatments to cure and actively prevent self-delusion:

1. Understanding the dangers of delusion

Learning about the consequences and effects of self-delusion encourages us to be aware and alert. Doing this helps us preserve and nurture any good that might be left within us to strive towards purification before it is too late to do so. There will come a time when some will beg for a second chance to make up for their flaws, but they will not be permitted:

$$حَتَّىٰٓ إِذَا جَآءَ أَحَدَهُمُ ٱلْمَوْتُ قَالَ رَبِّ ٱرْجِعُونِ ۞ لَعَلِّىٓ أَعْمَلُ صَٰلِحًا فِيمَا تَرَكْتُ ۚ كَلَّآ ۚ إِنَّهَا كَلِمَةٌ هُوَ قَآئِلُهَا ۖ وَمِن وَرَآئِهِم بَرْزَخٌ إِلَىٰ يَوْمِ يُبْعَثُونَ ۞$$

When death approaches any of them, they cry, "My Lord! Let me go back, so I may do good in what I left behind." Never! It is only a claim that they make. And there is a barrier behind them until the Day they are resurrected. [23:99-100]

2. Balance

Striving for balance in all that we do may sound abstract, but its effects are vast and deeply impactful. The importance of a holistic and balanced approach applies even to our worship and activism. This balance reduces the probability of self-delusion, and curbs the tendency to view our work as superior to the actions of others. The balanced path is one between zealous activism that we perform to increase our self-worth and inactivity.

Striking the Balance

It is beautiful to reflect upon how the Quranic word for moderation and middle, *wasat*, also means the best of something. To be balanced and moderate does not necessarily mean scaling back or reducing one's contribution—indeed, our standard for balance and moderation should be the Prophet ﷺ and his Companions. A person who seeks to apply balance and moderation in their life will be working toward the best possible outcomes in their activism, spirituality, character, career, and family life.

The very act of striving for balance is a humbling process that should counteract any self-admiration or conceit, for one must acknowledge their shortcomings and negative tendencies and work to counteract them. It requires knowledge of what is truly better and balanced, patience in making changes and remaining constant upon them, humility in acknowledging our flaws, and cooperation with others to elevate our implementation and awareness of ourselves.

3. Remembering the means of salvation

We must keep in mind at all times that our actions are not what will save us on the Day of Resurrection. We cannot rely on them. Our salvation will be purely from Allah's bounty and grace. This theme is repeated all throughout the Quran. Allah says, for example,

وَٱلَّذِينَ ءَامَنُواْ وَعَمِلُواْ ٱلصَّٰلِحَٰتِ سَنُدْخِلُهُمْ جَنَّٰتٍ تَجْرِى مِن تَحْتِهَا ٱلْأَنْهَٰرُ خَٰلِدِينَ فِيهَآ أَبَدًا لَّهُمْ فِيهَآ أَزْوَٰجٌ مُّطَهَّرَةٌ وَنُدْخِلُهُمْ ظِلًّا ظَلِيلًا ﴿﴾

As for those who believe and do good, We will admit them into Gardens under which rivers flow, to stay there forever. There they will have pure spouses, and We will place them under a vast shade. [4:57]

He also says,

وَأُدْخِلَ ٱلَّذِينَ ءَامَنُواْ وَعَمِلُواْ ٱلصَّٰلِحَٰتِ جَنَّٰتٍ تَجْرِى مِن تَحْتِهَا ٱلْأَنْهَٰرُ خَٰلِدِينَ فِيهَا بِإِذْنِ رَبِّهِمْ تَحِيَّتُهُمْ فِيهَا سَلَٰمٌ ۝

Those who believe and do good will be admitted into Gardens,
under which rivers flow—to stay there forever by the Will of their
Lord—where they will be greeted with "Peace!" [14:23]

And He says, highlighting that He is the One who will grant us entry into Paradise, rather than entrance relying on our own actions,

إِنَّ ٱللَّهَ يُدْخِلُ ٱلَّذِينَ ءَامَنُواْ وَعَمِلُواْ ٱلصَّٰلِحَٰتِ جَنَّٰتٍ تَجْرِى مِن تَحْتِهَا ٱلْأَنْهَٰرُ

Indeed, Allah will admit those who believe and do good into
Gardens, under which rivers flow. [22:14]

The Prophet ﷺ also made this clear to us when he said, *"No one's deeds will save him."*[25]

4. Learning the Quran and Sunnah

Constantly reading the book of Allah helps us better acquaint ourselves with the stories of the Prophets and their righteous followers. We will notice how fearful they were of succumbing to their own flaws. Despite this, they did not waver in their dedication to worship and good deeds, setting a model of balance and devotion for us all.

The Quran tells us about the story of Adam, for example, who took full responsibility for his mistake. He did not blame Satan, who goaded him on to eat from the forbidden tree, nor did he justify his action in any way; he desperately begged for forgiveness and mercy, exhibiting his weakness and dependance on Allah:

قَالَا رَبَّنَا ظَلَمْنَا أَنفُسَنَا وَإِن لَّمْ تَغْفِرْ لَنَا وَتَرْحَمْنَا لَنَكُونَنَّ مِنَ ٱلْخَٰسِرِينَ ۝

They said, "Our Lord! We have wronged ourselves. If You do not
forgive us and have mercy on us, we will certainly be losers." [7:23]

Prophet Noah also cried out to Allah with the same brokenness and desperation:

وَإِلَّا تَغْفِرْ لِى وَتَرْحَمْنِىٓ أَكُن مِّنَ ٱلْخَٰسِرِينَ ۝

"... and unless You forgive me and have mercy on me, I will be one of the losers." [11:47]

Prophet Abraham used these words to describe his Lord to the people,

وَٱلَّذِىٓ أَطْمَعُ أَن يَغْفِرَ لِى خَطِيٓئَتِى يَوْمَ ٱلدِّينِ ۝

"And He is the One Who, I hope, will forgive my flaws on Judgment Day." [26:82]

Likewise, the *seerah* (the biography of Prophet Muhammad ﷺ) is full of examples of humility, self-reproach, and holding oneself accountable. The study of the *seerah* is an indispensable resource for every Muslim in their knowledge and self-development, especially those who are actively working for the cause of Allah.

5. Reading the stories of the early Muslims

Learning about the Muslims in the early years of Islam and taking note of their intense focus on sincerity will help us put both the quality and the quantity of our own works into perspective. Rather than feeling safe or relying on their deeds for their salvation, they would actually suspect their actions of insufficiency. Reading about their humility and devotion to sincerity will inspire us to work harder to follow their example and avoid being deluded about our own deeds and piety.

Abu Bakr was the Prophet's ﷺ closest friend and—by unanimous agreement— the best human being to ever follow the Prophet Muhammad ﷺ. He had the most complete faith after the Prophet ﷺ. Despite this, he said about himself, "If the people knew my true state, they would bury me alive."

Likewise, when Imam al-Shāfi'i was nearing his own death, one of his companions asked him, "How are you doing?" This scholar, who was described by Imam Ahmad bin Hanbal as being "the light of this world and the source of God's security for all people," replied, "I am about to depart from this world, leave behind my brothers, meet my own sins, and stand in front of Allah; I do not know if He will order me into Paradise or into the Hellfire." Then he recited the poem:

Though my heavy heart weighs me down
and my veins are constricted
My hope in your mercy elevates me
Though my sins seem to exceed every boundary unrestricted
They cannot be compared to your boundless mercy

6. Structured learning and development

We have discussed previously how an imbalanced focus on learning secondary or highly technical matters can lead one to conceit. Focusing on the foundational matters of the religion and humbling ourselves to follow the path of learning that has been tread for centuries without taking any shortcuts can help us prevent a conceited, deluded personality. This methodical approach will also help us in making the most out of our time learning, benefitting ourselves and others with what we learn.

7. Avoiding conceited people

In order to prevent self-delusion, we must avoid spending too much time with people who are conceited. This, paired with spending more time with people who are conscious of Allah, who observe His boundaries at all times and who know the importance of doing good deeds while not relying on them for salvation, will serve as an effective remedy for all forms of self-admiration, delusion, and arrogance. These are all among the qualities of those whom Allah praises in the Quran:

إِنَّ ٱلَّذِينَ هُم مِّنْ خَشْيَةِ رَبِّهِم مُّشْفِقُونَ ۝ وَٱلَّذِينَ هُم بِـَٔايَٰتِ رَبِّهِمْ يُؤْمِنُونَ ۝ وَٱلَّذِينَ هُم بِرَبِّهِمْ لَا يُشْرِكُونَ ۝ وَٱلَّذِينَ يُؤْتُونَ مَآ ءَاتَوا۟ وَّقُلُوبُهُمْ وَجِلَةٌ أَنَّهُمْ إِلَىٰ رَبِّهِمْ رَٰجِعُونَ ۝ أُو۟لَٰٓئِكَ يُسَٰرِعُونَ فِى ٱلْخَيْرَٰتِ وَهُمْ لَهَا سَٰبِقُونَ ۝

Surely those who tremble in awe of their Lord, and who believe in
the revelations of their Lord, and who associate none with their
Lord, and who do whatever they do with their hearts fearful that
they will return to their Lord—it is they who race to do good deeds,
always taking the lead. [23:57-61]

8. Holding ourselves accountable

Self-awareness and keeping track of our actions and attitudes will alert us to when we are falling into delusion about ourselves. We must discipline ourselves through accountability and self-monitoring until we shed all of our bad habits. The Messenger of Allah ﷺ said,

> The intelligent is the one who takes account of himself and works for what comes after death. The incompetent is the one who lets himself follow his whims and has many hopes in Allah.[26]

9. Mentor support

Having others check up on us and fulfill their duty to us of good counsel is vital to our self development. We must know the correct methods of advising one another and have the will to give advice in the most appropriate way, even when uncomfortable. This can help us build a foolproof network of support that helps us all ward against falling into self-delusion.

10. Avoiding leadership when unprepared

Refraining from taking leadership positions until we are sure that we have the right qualifications and strategy for avoiding self-admiration and delusion is vital in our battle against this disease. If we do shun leadership, we should spend time developing our souls and nurturing humility, while also seeking other ways to serve and contribute to the field of Islamic work.

11. Proper etiquette for praise

We must also follow the correct guidelines that our religion sets for praising others. It is important to make sure that we are not engaging in the blameworthy forms of praise and flattery, especially toward public and influential figures who are highly susceptible to diseases of the self. Acceptable praise and compliments should be unexaggerated, truthful, specific, and designed to encourage good actions rather than vanity and complacency.

When praising good qualities in people, we should attribute them to Allah rather than the person by prefacing them with *masha'Allah* or *Alhamdulillah*. We should also avoid placing ourselves in a position where we become the object of excessive, unrestrained praise.

This weakens Satan's plan against us and helps us rid ourselves of any traces of conceit.

A Dua to Ward off Self-Admiration

Abu Bakr and other Companions used to say this dua' (supplication) whenever they were being praised:

اللَّهُمَّ اجْعَلْنِي خَيْرًا مِمَّا يَظُنُّونَ وَاغْفِرْ لِي مَا لَا
يَعْلَمُونَ وَلَا تُؤَاخِذْنِي بِمَا يَقُولُونَ

*Allahumm ij'alni khayran mimma yathunoon wa-ghfir lee ma la
ya'lamoon wa la tu'akhithni bi ma yaquloon*

Its meaning is: O Allah, make me better than what they think of
me, forgive me for what they do not know about me, and do not
blame me for what they say about me.

12. Encouraging others to do good openly

Actively encouraging others to share some of their good deeds and relate their experiences helps us and our communities appreciate one another more. We learn from the examples of others and find new role models and mentors to benefit from. This is especially effective for a population of youth who may feel superior and overly ambitious, while belittling the virtue of elders and leaders in their communities. Sharing some of our good deeds in public helps us encourage one another to do more and also see each other in a positive and respectful frame.

13. Fair treatment

Those in positions of leadership must be keen to treat everyone equally. The possibility of some community members developing conceited personalities due to favorable treatment was discussed previously. By promoting a culture in Islamic work that rejects favoritism and preferential treatment based on ethnicity, status, or pre-existing connections, we can bolster our collective immunity against so many diseases of the heart. We must ensure that we are not enabling Satan against each other.

14. Seeking God's help

Ultimately we must always ask Allah for help in all our endeavors, especially those of self-purification. He will never turn away anyone who seeks His assistance, and He will never let our efforts for His sake go to waste. He says,

$$\text{وَالَّذِينَ جَٰهَدُواْ فِينَا لَنَهْدِيَنَّهُمْ سُبُلَنَا ۚ وَإِنَّ ٱللَّهَ لَمَعَ ٱلْمُحْسِنِينَ ۝}$$

As for those who struggle in Our cause, We will surely guide them along Our Way. And Allah is certainly with the good-doers. [29:69]

It is a profound act of submission and reverence before Allah to acknowledge that we do not have power even over our own selves, without His permission and help. Without His guidance, we would fall victim to every disease of the self. Seeking help from Allah in our quest for self-purification is the first, middle and last step of overcoming any spiritual roadblocks in our way.

✦ ✦ ✦

ENDNOTES

1. Muslim, #55
2. Abu Dawud, #4918
3. al-Bukhari, v.7, p. 2 (in this wording); Muslim, #1401
4. Muslim, #2670
5. Ahmad, v. 1, p. 215, 347
6. al-Bukhari, v. 1, p. 16
7. Muslim, #2722
8. al-Bukhari, v. 4, p. 147; Muslim, #2989
9. al-Tirmidhi, #3175
10. al-Bukhari, v. 8, p. 122 (in this wording); Muslim, #2816, 2818
11. Fath al-Bari, v. 11, p. 105
12. al-Bukhari, v. 4, p. 41, 42
13. al-Tirmidhi, #3502
14. al-Bukhari, v. 8, p. 110
15. al-Ghazāli, Ihyā' 'Uloom al-Deen, v. 3, p. 207
16. al-Bukhari, v. 3, p. 64-65; Muslim, #2175
17. Abu Dawud, #575
18. Ihkām al-Ahkām, v. 2, p. 57
19. al-Bukhari, #v. 1, p. 165, 166; Muslim, #650
20. Muslim, #1017
21. al-Tirmidhi, al-Shamā'il al-Muⓩammadiyyah, p. 18-22 (as part of a longer hadith)
22. al-Bukhari, v. 1, p. 13, 14
23. al-Tirmidhi, #3253,
24. Abu Dawud, #4800
25. al-Bukhari, v. 8, p. 122 (in this wording); Muslim, #2816, 2818
26. Ibn Majah, #4260

Arrogance

Of the many challenges and roadblocks facing Islamic workers, perhaps the most serious and deadliest is arrogance. We must strive to purify ourselves from arrogance and protect ourselves from its spiritually lethal consequences. In this chapter, we will explore the roots of arrogance—its symptoms, causes, and effects, both individual and communal. Knowledge together with practice will help prevent the sincere Islamic worker from succumbing to this incapacitating disease.

The Arabic term for arrogance, *takabbur*, means to see oneself as great and to display that delusion in one's actions. Allah uses it in the Quran to describe those whom He punishes by turning them away from His revelation:

$$\text{سَأَصْرِفُ عَنْ ءَايَٰتِىَ ٱلَّذِينَ يَتَكَبَّرُونَ فِى ٱلْأَرْضِ بِغَيْرِ ٱلْحَقِّ}$$

I will turn away from My signs those who <u>act unjustly with arrogance</u> in the land. [7:146]

These are people who presume that they are the best of all creation, and think that they have distinctions and unique qualities that make them superior to others.

In our context of self-development in the field of Islamic work, we use the term more pointedly to describe a dangerous trait that even the most dedicated Islamic activists may be at risk for. *Takabbur* refers to the outward display of one's self-admiration and self-delusion in a way that is belittling of others. They wield an aura of superiority and infallibility over others. One who is afflicted with arrogance finds fault in everyone around him and takes advice from no one.

The Prophet ﷺ sternly warned us against the pitfalls and behaviors that lead to arrogance. Not only did he teach his Companions to purify themselves of arrogance, but he also defined it explicitly for them. He said, *"Whoever has a speck's weight of arrogance in his heart will not enter Paradise."* One man said, *"But someone might love for his garment and shoes to be nice."* The Prophet ﷺ responded, *"Allah is beautiful; He loves beauty. Arrogance is rejection of the truth and the belittlement of others."*[1]

We should make a point here to differentiate between arrogance and having a sense of honor and dignity. The difference between them should be clear; arrogance is a false sense of superiority while honor is a truthful consideration of what raises some above others. Arrogance is manifested through a denial and ingratitude of blessings, while honor is practiced through the acknowledgment of those blessings.

Causes of Arrogance

Given that self-admiration and delusion are diseases that, in their exacerbated forms, lead to increased belittlement of others and illusions of self-superiority, these three roadblocks share many of the same roots. Arrogance is the most advanced stage of self-admiration and delusion when they are untreated, allowed to ferment and grow unchecked. The following are some catalysts that might cause vanity and delusion about oneself to evolve into full-blown arrogance.

- *A Culture of low self-esteem*
- *Misplaced values*
- *Comparing our blessings to others*
- *Illusion of permanence*
- *Exceptional talent*
- *Ignoring the warnings against arrogance*

A CULTURE OF LOW SELF-ESTEEM

Interacting with others who have low self-esteem or excessive in their humility, to the point of self-abasement, may contribute to some individuals developing a sense of arrogance. Some people are excessively timid and humble, and refrain from offering their opinions or thoughts. They may even be too shy to step forward and fulfill their own responsibilities. Someone who falsely interprets these meek and reticent tendencies may mistake them for cowardice and inability. They compare the hesitation of others to their own confidence and initiative in taking on any challenge, looking down on those who appear to be less capable. With the encouraging whisperings of Satan, such a person will eventually develop a sense of superiority and disdain for others.

Allah draws our attention to this in the Quran through the teachings of His Messenger ﷺ. We find in both the Quran and the *sunnah* a general encouragement for all to speak of God's blessings upon them. Allah says, for example,

وَأَمَّا بِنِعْمَةِ رَبِّكَ فَحَدِّثْ ۞

And proclaim the blessings of your Lord. [93:11]

The Prophet ﷺ made clear that, *"Allah is beautiful; He loves beauty."*[2] He also prayed to Allah, saying, *"Make us grateful for your blessings, praising you for them and accepting of them. Complete them for us."*[3] These teachings help us avoid excessive timidity and secrecy in our community culture, allowing for the sharing of blessings and accomplishments within a healthy environment.

Malik bin Nadlah al-Jushami narrates that he once came to the Prophet ﷺ wearing ragged clothing. The Prophet ﷺ asked, *"Do you have any wealth?"* and he responded, *"Yes."* He asked, *"What kind of wealth?"* He said, *"Allah has given me some camels, sheep, horses, and servants."* The Prophet ﷺ then said, *"If Allah gives you wealth, the mark of Allah's blessings and grace should be seen on you."*[4]

The early generations of Muslims understood this concept well. They would often converse with their peers about the immense blessings that Allah bestowed upon them, and even call out those who would neglect to do so. Hasan bin Ali, the grandson of the

Prophet ﷺ, said, "If you receive or do good, then speak about it to your brothers whom you trust."[5] Bakr bin Abdullah al-Muzani also said, "Whoever is given good but it is not seen on him is then considered to be hated by Allah, and a transgressor with regards to Allah's blessings."[6]

MISPLACED VALUES

The catalyst for arrogance may be flawed standards in determining the worth of other people. Ignorance and materialism is prevalent in our communities, and so this leads people to assign more value to people of worldly accomplishments, even if their lifestyles are full of sin and far-detached from Allah's religion. All the while, society overlooks poor and modest people who wield scant worldly influence, despite their hard work and sincere dedication to Allah and His religion. Growing up amongst such corrupted standards can certainly affect our outlook, leading to an air of superiority and belittlement of other people.

The Quran contains many powerful reminders in which Allah recalibrates our world perspective. He abolishes these false standards and teaches us how to assign value correctly. For example, He says,

أَيَحْسَبُونَ أَنَّمَا نُمِدُّهُم بِهِۦ مِن مَّالٍ وَبَنِينَ ۝ نُسَارِعُ لَهُمْ فِى ٱلْخَيْرَٰتِ بَل لَّا يَشْعُرُونَ ۝

Do they think, since We provide them with wealth and children, that We hasten to them all kinds of good? No! They are not aware.
[23:55-56]

وَقَالُوا نَحْنُ أَكْثَرُ أَمْوَٰلًا وَأَوْلَٰدًا وَمَا نَحْنُ بِمُعَذَّبِينَ ۝ قُلْ إِنَّ رَبِّى يَبْسُطُ ٱلرِّزْقَ لِمَن يَشَآءُ وَيَقْدِرُ وَلَٰكِنَّ أَكْثَرَ ٱلنَّاسِ لَا يَعْلَمُونَ ۝ وَمَآ أَمْوَٰلُكُمْ وَلَآ أَوْلَٰدُكُم بِٱلَّتِى تُقَرِّبُكُمْ عِندَنَا زُلْفَىٰٓ إِلَّا مَنْ ءَامَنَ وَعَمِلَ صَٰلِحًا فَأُو۟لَٰٓئِكَ لَهُمْ جَزَآءُ ٱلضِّعْفِ بِمَا عَمِلُوا۟ وَهُمْ فِى ٱلْغُرُفَٰتِ ءَامِنُونَ ۝

They said, "We are far superior in wealth and children, and we will never be punished." Say, "Surely my Lord gives abundant or limited provisions to whoever He wills. But most people do not know." It is not your wealth or children that bring you closer to Us. But those who believe and do good—it is they who will have a multiplied

reward for what they did, and they will be secure in mansions.
[34:35-37]

The Messenger of Allah saw a man pass by, so he ﷺ asked the companion who was sitting next to him: "What is your opinion of that man?" His Companion responded: "He is one of the most noble of all people. This man—by Allah!—is worthy to be married if he proposes, and is worthy of his intercession to be accepted if he intercedes." The Messenger of Allah ﷺ fell silent. Another man then passed, and the Messenger of Allah ﷺ asked: "What is your opinion of this man?" He said: "O Messenger of Allah, this man is one of the poor Muslims. This man would probably not be married if he proposed. His intercession would not be accepted nor would his opinion be considered if he spoke up." The Messenger of Allah ﷺ said: *"This one man is better than an earth full of the other man."*[7]

COMPARING OUR BLESSINGS TO OTHERS

We may also fall into arrogance by constantly comparing our blessings to those of others, forgetting the Source of All Blessings. Allah might very well give some blessings to one person that He does not give to another, but it is all from His divine wisdom. Some are healthy while others suffer, some are married with children while others may be struggling to find a spouse or conceive. Allah may bless one person with captivating charm and popularity while leaving someone else obscured in the shadows.

While everyone pays mind to the manifestations of these blessings, openly or covertly judging who deserves what, they forget that each blessing came from Allah. He chose with calculated and deliberate wisdom what goes to whom. When we assume that we got less than we deserve, or that someone else may have received more than their virtues warrant, we are committing a grave and dangerous form of arrogance.

Allah addresses this attitude in the Quran at length. He tells us one story about a man blessed with much wealth and luxury. When he compared his blessings to that of his friend, he saw that his friend had much less wealth to show for himself, so he assumed that his own blessings were deserved and hard-earned. God says,

وَٱضۡرِبۡ لَهُم مَّثَلًا رَّجُلَيۡنِ جَعَلۡنَا لِأَحَدِهِمَا جَنَّتَيۡنِ مِنۡ أَعۡنَٰبٍ وَحَفَفۡنَٰهُمَا بِنَخۡلٍ وَجَعَلۡنَا بَيۡنَهُمَا زَرۡعًا ۝ كِلۡتَا ٱلۡجَنَّتَيۡنِ ءَاتَتۡ أُكُلَهَا وَلَمۡ تَظۡلِم مِّنۡهُ شَيۡـًٔا ۚ وَفَجَّرۡنَا خِلَٰلَهُمَا نَهَرًا ۝ وَكَانَ لَهُۥ ثَمَرٌ فَقَالَ لِصَٰحِبِهِۦ وَهُوَ يُحَاوِرُهُۥٓ أَنَا۠ أَكۡثَرُ مِنكَ مَالًا وَأَعَزُّ نَفَرًا ۝

Give them an example of two men. To one We gave two gardens of grapevines, which We surrounded with palm trees and placed crops in between. Each garden yielded its produce, never falling short. And We caused a river to flow between them.

And he had other resources. So he boasted to a companion of his, while conversing with him, "I am greater than you in wealth and superior in manpower." [18:32-34]

The verses continue on to recount how the man with less wealth warned that worldly status and comfort is not necessarily an indicator of status in God's sight. When the wealthy man didn't pay heed, God destroyed his property and stripped him of all he took pride in.

THE ILLUSION OF PERMANENCE

Another reason that we might become arrogant is that we assume that our blessings will never be lost. We become heady and over-confident in what we have: skills, belongings, popularity, intelligence, or otherwise. Some people become so engrossed in their blessings that they never consider the possibility that one day they might not be there. This illusion of permanence results in a false sense of reality.

The man from the previously mentioned story of the two gardens explicitly expressed this. Allah tells us,

وَدَخَلَ جَنَّتَهُۥ وَهُوَ ظَالِمٌ لِّنَفۡسِهِۦ قَالَ مَآ أَظُنُّ أَن تَبِيدَ هَٰذِهِۦٓ أَبَدًا ۝ وَمَآ أَظُنُّ ٱلسَّاعَةَ قَآئِمَةً وَلَئِن رُّدِدتُّ إِلَىٰ رَبِّي لَأَجِدَنَّ خَيۡرًا مِّنۡهَا مُنقَلَبًا ۝

And he entered his property, while wronging his soul, saying, "I do not think this will ever perish, nor do I think the Hour will come. And if in fact I am returned to my Lord, I will definitely get a far better outcome than all this." [18:35-36]

Allah also informs us that this phenomenon is widespread among us humans:

$$\text{وَلَئِنْ أَذَقْنَهُ رَحْمَةً مِّنَّا مِنْ بَعْدِ ضَرَّآءَ مَسَّتْهُ لَيَقُولَنَّ هَذَا لِى وَمَآ أَظُنُّ}$$

$$\text{ٱلسَّاعَةَ قَآئِمَةً وَلَئِن رُّجِعْتُ إِلَىٰ رَبِّىٓ إِنَّ لِى عِندَهُ لَلْحُسْنَىٰ}$$

*And if We let them taste a mercy from Us after being touched with
adversity, they will certainly say, "This is what I deserve. I do not
think the Hour will ever come. And if in fact I am returned to my
Lord, the finest reward with Him will definitely be mine." [41:50]*

EXCEPTIONAL TALENT

Standing out in one's knowledge, public speaking, leadership, cre-
ativity, or other abilities in the field of Islamic work can certainly
lead to arrogance. Allah chooses to bless some before others in these
matters, and arrogance begins to take root when they begin to see
a talent as grounds for their own superiority and entitlement. They
may even begin to see themselves as irreplaceable, the source of all
success within a team or an organization. They tell themselves, "if it
wasn't for me, we wouldn't have achieved such and such."

Allah calls our attention to this root cause of arrogance in the
Quran—He teaches us that impressive contributions are worthless
without sincerity. He says,

$$\text{وَٱلسَّٰبِقُونَ ٱلْأَوَّلُونَ مِنَ ٱلْمُهَٰجِرِينَ وَٱلْأَنصَارِ وَٱلَّذِينَ ٱتَّبَعُوهُم بِإِحْسَٰنٍ}$$

$$\text{رَّضِىَ ٱللَّهُ عَنْهُمْ وَرَضُواْ عَنْهُ وَأَعَدَّ لَهُمْ جَنَّٰتٍ تَجْرِى تَحْتَهَا ٱلْأَنْهَٰرُ خَٰلِدِينَ}$$

$$\text{فِيهَآ أَبَدًا ذَٰلِكَ ٱلْفَوْزُ ٱلْعَظِيمُ ۞}$$

*As for the foremost—the first of the Emigrants and the Helpers—
and those who follow them in goodness, Allah is pleased with them
and they are pleased with Him. And He has prepared for them
Gardens under which rivers flow, to stay there forever and ever.
That is the ultimate triumph. [9:100]*

He also says,

$$\text{لِلْفُقَرَآءِ ٱلْمُهَٰجِرِينَ ٱلَّذِينَ أُخْرِجُواْ مِن دِيَٰرِهِمْ وَأَمْوَٰلِهِمْ يَبْتَغُونَ فَضْلًا مِّنَ}$$

$$\text{ٱللَّهِ وَرِضْوَٰنًا وَيَنصُرُونَ ٱللَّهَ وَرَسُولَهُ أُوْلَٰٓئِكَ هُمُ ٱلصَّٰدِقُونَ ۞ وَٱلَّذِينَ}$$

$$\text{تَبَوَّءُو ٱلدَّارَ وَٱلْإِيمَٰنَ مِن قَبْلِهِمْ يُحِبُّونَ مَنْ هَاجَرَ إِلَيْهِمْ وَلَا يَجِدُونَ فِى}$$

$$\text{صُدُورِهِمْ حَاجَةً مِّمَّآ أُوتُواْ وَيُؤْثِرُونَ عَلَىٰٓ أَنفُسِهِمْ وَلَوْ كَانَ بِهِمْ خَصَاصَةٌ}$$

وَمَن يُوقَ شُحَّ نَفْسِهِۦ فَأُو۟لَٰٓئِكَ هُمُ ٱلْمُفْلِحُونَ ۝ وَٱلَّذِينَ جَآءُو مِنۢ
بَعْدِهِمْ يَقُولُونَ رَبَّنَا ٱغْفِرْ لَنَا وَلِإِخْوَٰنِنَا ٱلَّذِينَ سَبَقُونَا بِٱلْإِيمَٰنِ وَلَا تَجْعَلْ
فِى قُلُوبِنَا غِلًّا لِّلَّذِينَ ءَامَنُوا۟ رَبَّنَآ إِنَّكَ رَءُوفٌ رَّحِيمٌ ۝

It is for poor emigrants who were driven out of their homes and
wealth, seeking Allah's bounty and pleasure, and standing up for
Allah and His Messenger. They are the ones true in faith.

As for those who had settled in the city and the faith before the
emigrants, they love whoever immigrates to them, never having a
desire in their hearts for whatever is given to the emigrants. They
give preference over themselves even though they may be in need.
And whoever is saved from the selfishness of their own souls, it is
they who are successful.

And those who come after them will pray, "Our Lord! Forgive us
and our fellow believers who preceded us in faith, and do not allow
bitterness into our hearts towards those who believe. Our Lord!
Indeed, You are Ever Gracious, Most Merciful." [59:8-10]

The reason that the *Muhajiroon*, the emigrants from Makkah to
Madinah, had precedence over others in the sight of Allah was due
to their unparalleled sincerity in their actions and their devotion to
the truth. There is a saying that goes, "Honor is not for the forerun-
ners, but for the sincere." Their migration in and of itself was a test
of faith that no one after them had to endure.

The same goes for the *Ansar*, the Helpers, who fully embraced the
Muhajiroon, welcoming them into their homes and supporting them
with their resources. These two groups are distinguished for their
extraordinary actions, not due to the scale of the action itself, but
because along with their actions came exceptional sincerity. Thus,
Allah says,

مِنَ ٱلْمُؤْمِنِينَ رِجَالٌ صَدَقُوا۟ مَا عَٰهَدُوا۟ ٱللَّهَ عَلَيْهِ فَمِنْهُم مَّن قَضَىٰ نَحْبَهُۥ
وَمِنْهُم مَّن يَنتَظِرُ وَمَا بَدَّلُوا۟ تَبْدِيلًا ۝

Among the believers are men who have proven true to what they
pledged to Allah. Some of them have fulfilled their pledge, and
others are waiting. They have never changed anything in the least.
[33:23]

IGNORANCE OF THE DANGERS OF ARROGANCE

Being oblivious to the dangerous consequences of arrogance and neglecting to monitor one's level of sincerity can result in a lowering of our guard, which provides an opening for devilish whisperings to embed themselves in our mind and heart. Anyone who is unaware of the harms of any disease is at higher risk of exposing themselves to it. Because they do not know the symptoms, they may end up diagnosing their illness only after it is too late to effectively treat.

Symptoms of Arrogance

If we are sincere in seeking Allah's pleasure and company, we should be on a sharp lookout for anything in our character that displeases Him. There are a number of symptoms we can look for to determine whether we might be afflicted with arrogance.

CARRYING ONESELF POMPOUSLY

Displaying ostentation in your gait, turning away when you are given advice or words of truth, and carrying a contemptuous demeanor are blaring signals of arrogance. Allah warns us in the Quran against displaying these pompous behaviors to those around us. He criticizes and threatens those who, when they are presented with revelation,

$$ثَانِىَ عِطْفِهِ لِيُضِلَّ عَن سَبِيلِ ٱللَّهِ$$

They turn a stiff neck away in order to divert away from God's path.
[22:9]

And He teaches us through the lessons that the wise Luqman teaches to his son,

$$وَلَا تُصَعِّرْ خَدَّكَ لِلنَّاسِ وَلَا تَمْشِ فِى ٱلْأَرْضِ مَرَحًا إِنَّ ٱللَّهَ لَا يُحِبُّ كُلَّ مُخْتَالٍ فَخُورٍ ۞$$

"And do not turn your nose up to people nor walk pridefully upon the earth. Surely Allah does not like whoever is arrogant, boastful."
[31:18]

He also repeats,

$$وَٱللَّهُ لَا يُحِبُّ كُلَّ مُخْتَالٍ فَخُورٍ$$

For Allah does not like whoever is arrogant, boastful [57:23]

CAUSING TURMOIL

Causing trouble and turmoil at every opportunity to do so is also indicative of arrogance. Arrogant people will usually reject counsel or criticism from anyone and look down upon the truth when it does not affirm their own superiority. Allah warns us against those who have these traits,

$$وَمِنَ ٱلنَّاسِ مَن يُعْجِبُكَ قَوْلُهُ فِى ٱلْحَيَوٰةِ ٱلدُّنْيَا وَيُشْهِدُ ٱللَّهَ عَلَىٰ مَا فِى قَلْبِهِۦ وَهُوَ أَلَدُّ ٱلْخِصَامِ ۝ وَإِذَا تَوَلَّىٰ سَعَىٰ فِى ٱلْأَرْضِ لِيُفْسِدَ فِيهَا وَيُهْلِكَ ٱلْحَرْثَ وَٱلنَّسْلَ وَٱللَّهُ لَا يُحِبُّ ٱلْفَسَادَ ۝ وَإِذَا قِيلَ لَهُ ٱتَّقِ ٱللَّهَ أَخَذَتْهُ ٱلْعِزَّةُ بِٱلْإِثْمِ$$

There are some who impress you with their views regarding worldly affairs and openly call upon Allah to witness what is in their hearts, yet they are your worst adversaries. And when they leave, they strive throughout the land to spread mischief in it and destroy crops and cattle. And Allah does not like mischief. When it is said to them, "Fear Allah," pride carries them off to sin. [2:204-206]

EXCESSIVE TALK

Speaking too much can be a sign of arrogance. This applies especially to those who are eloquent and articulate in their speech. The Prophet ﷺ said, *"Allah, Mighty and Majestic, despises the eloquent among men who rolls his tongue like a cow does."*[8] He also made the connection between speaking excessively and self-centeredness—people who talk too much tend to shift the focus of the conversation to themselves. He ﷺ said, *"May I tell you about the worst ones among you? They are the ones who prattle on and brag."*[9]

SPECIFIC FASHIONS

Certain mannerisms in dress may also indicate a growing sense of arrogance. The Arabs at the time of the Prophet ﷺ would let their clothing drag on the ground as a display of their excess wealth. The Prophet ﷺ warned against this explicitly, saying, *"Whoever drags his garment out of pride, then Allah will not look at Him on the Day of Resurrection."* Abu Bakr said, *"But one side of my lower garment trails down, even though I keep trying to stop it."* The Prophet ﷺ said, *"You are not one of those who does it out of pride."*[10] Although long, draping garments may not be a display of ostentation and status in our context, there are other mannerisms and forms of dress that may be symptomatic of prideful intentions. It is worth contemplating about what these mannerisms might be and doing our best to avoid them.

SEEKING ATTENTION

If we persistently call attention to ourselves, this may indicate a desire for others to recognize our perceived status or superiority. This is especially troublesome when we enjoy receiving attention but resent giving attention to anyone else. Arrogance may also take the form of relishing when people acknowledge your presence through certain gestures, such as standing up for you when you enter a room. The Prophet ﷺ threatened anyone with this quality, saying, *"Whoever loves that others stand for him should prepare his seat in the Hellfire."*[11] Arrogance can also manifest as an eagerness to be in front of a crowd, the star of a gathering, or the first to speak.

Effects of Arrogance

Arrogance has devastating effects on the individual, the community, and the work that they do. Like all of the roadblocks and diseases discussed in this book, the harm extends beyond the individual's heart to the community and the progress of Islamic work, hindering the fulfilment of our mission on earth. Some individual effects are as follows:

BEING DEPRIVED OF INSIGHT

Arrogance can deprive a person of proper insight. Because they see themselves as higher and better than others, they end up not seeing many things from the perspectives of others. You will find that many arrogant people fail to appreciate or take heed of Allah's signs all throughout the universe and within themselves. Allahs says,

وَكَأَيِّن مِّنْ ءَايَةٍ فِى ٱلسَّمَـٰوَٰتِ وَٱلْأَرْضِ يَمُرُّونَ عَلَيْهَا وَهُمْ عَنْهَا مُعْرِضُونَ ۝

How many signs in the heavens and the earth do they pass by with indifference! [12:105]

Anyone indifferent to the perspectives of others and blinded to their own internal reflections is at a great loss. They will only persist in their flaws and mistakes, digging deeper into their errant ways until it is too late. When the Prophet ﷺ received the following verses of revelation, he spent the night shedding tears contemplating them:

إِنَّ فِى خَلْقِ ٱلسَّمَـٰوَٰتِ وَٱلْأَرْضِ وَٱخْتِلَـٰفِ ٱلَّيْلِ وَٱلنَّهَارِ لَـَٔايَـٰتٍ لِّأُو۟لِى ٱلْأَلْبَـٰبِ ۝ ٱلَّذِينَ يَذْكُرُونَ ٱللَّهَ قِيَـٰمًا وَقُعُودًا وَعَلَىٰ جُنُوبِهِمْ وَيَتَفَكَّرُونَ فِى خَلْقِ ٱلسَّمَـٰوَٰتِ وَٱلْأَرْضِ رَبَّنَا مَا خَلَقْتَ هَـٰذَا بَـٰطِلًا سُبْحَـٰنَكَ فَقِنَا عَذَابَ ٱلنَّارِ ۝

Indeed, in the creation of the heavens and the earth and the alternation of the day and night there are signs for people of reason—those who remember Allah while standing, sitting, and lying on their sides, and reflect on the creation of the heavens and the earth. "Our Lord! You have not created this without purpose. Glory be to You! Protect us from the torment of the Fire." [3:190-191]

He said about them, *"Doomed is whoever recites these ayahs and does not reflect over them."*[12] Allah warns in the Quran,

سَأَصْرِفُ عَنْ ءَايَـٰتِىَ ٱلَّذِينَ يَتَكَبَّرُونَ فِى ٱلْأَرْضِ بِغَيْرِ ٱلْحَقِّ

I will turn away from My signs those who act unjustly with arrogance in the land. [7:146]

INNER ANXIETY

Arrogance creates an internal state of unease and discomfort. In order to satisfy their need for perfection and superiority, arrogant people feed off of the attention and approval of others. This creates an internal dependency on others that can only lead to anxiety and unpredictable emotions. At the same time that arrogant people look to others for feedback on their own prestige, they require admiration to come from people who are beneath them, not from the same plane.

Because the most noble and honorable people usually refuse to give their attention to those who actively seek it out, this leaves the arrogant people uneasy and insecure. Arrogant people spend so much time, effort, and mental energy trying to craft a particular image of themselves that they forget about Allah. The most mild consequence of this is a feeling of inner sadness and insecurity. For the believer, Allah is the source of stability and confidence, and the arrogant person loses this secure foundation. Allah says,

وَمَنْ أَعْرَضَ عَن ذِكْرِى فَإِنَّ لَهُ مَعِيشَةً ضَنكًا

But whoever turns away from My Reminder will certainly have a miserable life... [20:124]

Allah also says,

وَمَن يُعْرِضْ عَن ذِكْرِ رَبِّهِ يَسْلُكْهُ عَذَابًا صَعَدًا ۝

And whoever turns away from the remembrance of their Lord will be admitted by Him into an overwhelming punishment. [72:17]

NEWLY EMBEDDED FLAWS

The third effect that comes from being arrogant is the introduction of new flaws and shortcomings. This is because those who are arrogant don't bother to assess themselves, since they are already convinced of their superiority. They do not examine the extent of their own weaknesses and the limitations of their strengths, glossing over advice or criticism that might help them grow. Someone like this will be inundated with more and more flaws, oblivious of their presence until they are fully embedded in their character, and it is too late to address them.

Allah draws our attention to this terrifying possibility of not being aware of our own faults. He says,

قُلْ هَلْ نُنَبِّئُكُم بِٱلْأَخْسَرِينَ أَعْمَلًا ۝ ٱلَّذِينَ ضَلَّ سَعْيُهُمْ فِى ٱلْحَيَوٰةِ ٱلدُّنْيَا

وَهُمْ يَحْسَبُونَ أَنَّهُمْ يُحْسِنُونَ صُنْعًا ۝

*Say, "Shall we inform you of who will lose the most deeds? Those
whose efforts are in vain in this worldly life, while they think they
are doing good."* [18:103-104]

He also says,

بَلَىٰ مَن كَسَبَ سَيِّئَةً وَأَحَٰطَتْ بِهِۦ خَطِيٓـَٔتُهُۥ فَأُوْلَٰٓئِكَ أَصْحَٰبُ ٱلنَّارِ هُمْ
فِيهَا خَٰلِدُونَ ۝

*But no! Those who commit evil and are engrossed in sin will be the
residents of the Fire. They will be there forever.* [2:81]

BARRED FROM PARADISE

The ultimate damage that arrogance can do to an individual is preventing their entrance into Paradise. Considering yourself to be better
than other human beings is to consider yourself to be divine, and
such an abhorrent assumption leads to great evil.

Depending on the severity of the arrogance within a person, and
whether they follow Islam at all, Allah will either punish them for
a limited time or forever. Allah says in a *hadith qudsi*, wherein the
Prophet ﷺ quotes God directly, *"Pride is my upper-garment, and
grandeur is my lower-garment. I will throw whoever vies with me
for either of them into Hell."*[13] The Prophet ﷺ also warned us clearly
that, *"No one with a speck's weight of arrogance in his heart will
enter Paradise."*[14] And he said, *"Shall I inform you of the People of
the Hellfire? Every aggressive, greedy, and prideful person."*[15]

CAUSING DIVISION

The arrogance of individuals can also be a detriment to the impact
and success of the entire community. Human hearts are drawn to
those who treat them kindly and act humbly, and we tend to dislike those who consider themselves better than us and who belittle
us. We avoid such arrogant people and will do anything to keep a
distance from them. This results in the arrogant person being abandoned without many who are willing to support him or her, leading
to feelings of abandonment, depression, and malice. This can cause
division within and between organizations.

When an Islamic movement is torn and divided from within, it is easy to defeat. It is rendered ineffective and unsuccessful, as no real results can be produced in such an environment. Allah draws our attention to this in the Quran, when He describes the hypocrites:

$$وَرَأَيْتَهُمْ يَصُدُّونَ وَهُم مُّسْتَكْبِرُونَ ۝$$

... and you see them turn away in arrogance. [63:5]?

The Prophet ﷺ said, *"Allah revealed to me that you must stay humble, so that no one feels proud over another, and no one transgresses against another."*[16]

BEING DEPRIVED OF ALLAH'S AID

Allah has shown us through past examples that He only extends His divine aid and assistance to those who subdue their egos and strip themselves of Satan's grasp. These sincere individuals and groups don't live for themselves, but rather for Allah. Arrogant people, however, feed and worship their own egos and thus have no right to Allah's divine aid and assistance. This is perhaps one of the lessons we can infer from the verse,

$$وَلَقَدْ نَصَرَكُمُ اللَّهُ بِبَدْرٍ وَأَنتُمْ أَذِلَّةٌ$$

Indeed, Allah made you victorious at Badr when you were humble.
[3:123]

Allah tied His victory to their humble and weak state. It seems that when this component of humility is lost within someone working for Islam, God's help is withdrawn.

Cures for Arrogance

If we have found any trace of arrogance within ourselves, we must strive to purify ourselves completely. Those of us who may only have some whisperings of self-admiration must still take every precaution to not fall into arrogance. The following 14 points are treatments for arrogance and methods of preventing it:

1. Remembering the dangers

Reminding ourselves of the harmful consequences of arrogance helps us to stay alert. We should read and educate ourselves about all spiritual roadblocks and diseases, their symptoms, effects, and preventions. We must always keep in mind the dangers that arrogance poses to both the soul on an individual level and the work on an organizational level. These harms hurt us in this life and the next, as we have shown, and reminding ourselves of this can perhaps keep us aware of any potential threat of arrogance within us, as well as give us the energy to actively prevent it in ourselves and others.

2. Visiting the sick

Frequent visits to those who are sick can help us against any potential arrogance we might have. Spending time with people who are on the verge of death, or who have been severely tested in any way, is humbling and can remind us of the nature of life and our own selves. Attending funerals and visiting graves also have the same bolstering effect on spirituality and character. These exceptional experiences shock us into returning to our Lord with humility and brokenness.

3. Avoiding the arrogant

Choosing to avoid self-centered, pompous people is also effective in preventing our own arrogance. The arrogance within them may spread to us over time. If we do not limit our exposure to negative characteristics, the darkness within others will overwhelm any light we might still have ourselves.

4. Spending time with the poor

Attending gatherings and taking the time to visit and serve people who are disadvantaged and in need is also a powerful way for us to stay humble. Spending casual time eating and drinking with those who have less material wealth and less influence than we do keeps us grateful and mindful of Allah, the source of all blessings. This is what the Prophet ﷺ used to do, along with his Companions and the righteous scholars after them. Once again, we see how Allah's religion connects our own spirituality and self-development with the wellbeing of the community and the upholding of social bonds.

5. Continuous reflection

Reflecting on the soul, the universe, and all of the blessings surrounding us will certainly humble us. We must ask ourselves and constantly remind ourselves of the resounding answers to these questions: Who created all of this? Who is sustaining it all? What did we do to deserve it, and what would it be like if we lost any of it? This line of thinking and contemplation activates our humility and gratitude, and helps us realize the imminent threat of losing our blessings. It will also drive us to urgently repent and return to Allah.

6. Heeding stories about arrogant people

Hearing or reading about the stories of the arrogant, paying special attention to their bitter ends, is an effective antidote against arrogance. There are many examples, beginning with the story of Satan himself, and continuing with the tyrants like Nimrod and Pharaoh, and their assistants like Hāmān and Qāroon. There are examples all throughout the life story of the Prophet ﷺ, such as Abu Jahl, Ubay bin Khalaf, and Abu Lahab. Reading through history all the way up until our current times will show that there was no society or era that was free of arrogant antagonists, and God made examples of all of them. Realizing this will inspire a healthy fear and caution in our hearts and remind us to urgently return to Him.

7. Attending gatherings of knowledge

Taking part in classes and discussion groups in our communities and spending time with knowledgeable people who are trustworthy and aware of the soul's discipline can help keep our spiritual health and character intact. Such gatherings will soften our heart, and will be full of individuals who may alert and help us if we are struggling with vices. Knowledge restores life to souls crippled by ignorance.

8. Doing what others avoid

Forcing ourselves to do what others would grumble at (as long as it is Islamically permissible) is an effective way to fight off arrogance. This is a powerful form of self-discipline. We can begin by making sure we do all of our own tasks and chores ourselves, even if we can afford to hire or request others to do them. This includes simple tasks like buying our groceries and cooking our own food, as well as more laborious chores like cleaning and housework. This is directly following the example of the Prophet ﷺ, his Companions, and their successors. This is a potent form of refining and disciplining our souls and returning them to their original humble form.

9. Apologizing

Owning up to our past mistakes and transgressions against others by directly asking them for forgiveness can help us defeat any traces of arrogance within us. We should seek out those whom we may have hurt and unreluctantly apologize to them for the pain we have caused them, validating their feelings and never justifying or deflecting the blame for our wrongdoings. We should also offer them any means of rectification when appropriate. We can learn from the example of Abu Dharr, who, after insulting Bilal, attempted to right his mistake by planting his face into the dirt and insisting that Bilal accept due rectification from him.

10. Noticing and mentioning the blessings of others

Pointing out the positive qualities and gifts that Allah has bestowed on others can help us combat and prevent arrogance within ourselves. While we may assume that every one recognizes that their blessings come from Allah, sometimes the arrogant person needs a tangible reminder of the source of their gifts. It is hoped that they will see the good in others and begin to humble themselves as a result.

11. Remembering the true standard of virtue

We must always remember the standard through which Allah ranks His servants—the standard that eradicated all others. Allah says,

$$ \text{إِنَّ أَكْرَمَكُمْ عِندَ ٱللَّهِ أَتْقَىٰكُمْ} $$

Surely the most noble of you in the sight of Allah is the most righteous among you.[49:13]

The Prophet ﷺ also emphasized the true standard when he proclaimed, *"All of you are children of Adam, and Adam was created from soil. Any people who take pride in their ancestry must stop, or else they will become less significant to Allah, the Exalted, than a dung beetle."*[17]

12. Consistent worship

The ritual acts of worship are powerful in extinguishing any evil residue from our souls. But this is only true when they are performed consistently and correctly with sincere intentions. Through worship, the soul rises into the highest levels of existence, continuously shedding the weight of worldly attachments. With our good deeds we cut the ropes of any anchors that may be keeping us from our ascension towards Allah. As Allah promises,

$$مَنْ عَمِلَ صَلِحًا مِّن ذَكَرٍ أَوْ أُنثَىٰ وَهُوَ مُؤْمِنٌ فَلَنُحْيِيَنَّهُ حَيَوٰةً طَيِّبَةً$$

Whoever does good, whether male or female, and is a believer, We will surely bless them with a good life [16:97]

13. Holding ourselves accountable

Taking account of ourselves in regards to our outer and inner actions helps us stay on track with our priorities. We are also able to know the extent to which the disease of arrogance may have spread into our hearts and come up with a strategy to uproot it. We are able to define our strengths and our weaknesses, and develop the former while defeating the latter.

14. Asking Allah for help

Begging God for his assistance is vital for defeating the arrogance within us. He is the only one who can help us ultimately defeat the disease. Fortunately for us, He is there to answer every call:

$$أَمَّن يُجِيبُ الْمُضْطَرَّ إِذَا دَعَاهُ وَيَكْشِفُ السُّوٓءَ وَيَجْعَلُكُمْ خُلَفَآءَ الْأَرْضِ ۗ أَءِلَهٌ مَّعَ اللَّهِ ۚ قَلِيلًا مَّا تَذَكَّرُونَ ۞$$

Or who responds to the distressed when they cry to Him, relieving affliction, and who makes you successors in the earth? Is it another god besides Allah? How little you remember! [27:62]

✦ ✦ ✦

ENDNOTES

1. Muslim, #91
2. Ibid.
3. Tafsir Ibn Kathir, v. 4, p. 523
4. Abu Dawud, #4063
5. al-Qurtubi, al-Jāmi' li'Ahkām al-Qur'ān, v. 20, p. 102
6. Ibid.
7. al-Bukhari, #6447
8. Abu Dawud, #5005
9. Ahmad, v. 19, p. 76
10. Abu Dawud, #4085
11. Abu Dawud, #5229
12. Tafseer Ibn Kathir, v. 1, pp. 440, 441
13. Ibn Majah, #4174
14. Muslim, #91
15. al-Bukhari, v. 8, p. 24
16. Muslim, #2865
17. Tafseer Ibn Kathir, v. 4, p. 217

Made in the USA
Middletown, DE
22 December 2021